MY TIME AT SEA

By

Eden S. Mathews
(aka Tony)

DAVID.
HOPE YOU ENJOY THIS
SNAPSHOT OF MY TIMES.

Tony

To Dot, whose selfless love,
loyalty and support has meant so
much.

To the kids, Sue, Jenny, Diane
and Peter, who have all been such
fun.

First Published 2010 by Appin Press, an imprint of Countyvise Ltd.
14 Appin Road, Birkenhead, Wirral CH41 9HH

Copyright © 2010 Eden S. Mathews

The right of Eden S. Mathews to be identified as the author of this work has been asserted by him in accordance with the Copyright, Design and Patents Act 1988.

British Library Cataloguing in Publication Data.

A catalogue record for this book is available from the British Library.

ISBN 978 1 906205 44 7

Prologue

This book is not just about me. It is about what I experienced, saw and shared. Seafaring is about a group of strangers put together for a few months and sent off out into the wide world. This book is about what we did, where we were, why we were there, what we thought.

This book started because, like many travellers, I took some photos. I don't pretend to be a keen photographer. To begin with I had a basic 'Kodak 101' which produced small black and white prints. Later I elevated to the 'Kodak Colorsnap'. This produced colour slides. These looked very nice, but to see them you needed a screen and projector. So they stayed in the box for a few years. In recent times, technology became available to the masses. After many experiments and enquiries, I was able to scan and print from the negatives, and I was very pleasantly surprised with the quality and colour of the slides. So a number of photos were printed. Then the question arose 'so what?' There was only one person who knew what they were about, so I added text. 'this is a seagull' etc. This had its limitations, so I decided to write about the background, and created display books.

As an Old Conway I have been attending the annual dinner over the last few years. Here I became aware of others who have written about different things, that not everybody became Admirals or Captains of the QE 2, but that there was an interest in recent history. So I have followed that through. As this book is mainly about my seagoing experiences, the first part 'My Childhood' is at the back, even though there are some voyages in it.

I have not dwelt on the discomfort, extreme conditions, broken sleep, extended work hours, uncooperative labour, or the constant dangers. Here's hoping that you enjoy the special situations, the companionship and above all, the love, respect, and special fellowship of the sea.

Acknowledgements

With grateful thanks to those who wittingly, or unwittingly, have helped through enthusiasm, or interest, to encourage me to write this book.

Conway Club members:
Beaumont, Capt. Jack & Janet
Hollinrake, Margaret
Johnston, Capt. Ian & Lucy
Kitching, Capt. Bill & Meg
McManus, Capt. Brian
Nutman, Capt. David
Windsor, Alfie

Evans, Paul
Davidson, Lyn. Memoir club
Emmerson, John & Jean (Countyvise)
Seston, Terry & Babs
Stanton, Kent & Pam
Stanton, Robbie
Tart, Derek & Marion

Beaumont House old boys
Geest Passenger Services
Friends and companions, whose subtle wisdom helped me through the complexities of modern technology.

Contents

PART ONE

First Time at Sea

Age 14-23

MY TIME AT SEA

2

HMS Conway

April 1951

The journey would take all day. Train from Tunbridge Wells to London, then Euston to Bangor. You had to be in uniform, and you took your own sandwiches. The train stopped at all the main stations, and after a while the novelty would wear off. Other cadets would join, but you didn't know anyone, and they seemed to go to other parts of the train. Arrival after 1730, here we were met with double decker buses. We quickly loaded our cases and set off to the school. It was a grey, dark, and drizzly evening. We unloaded, and were allocated our 'Tops' and dormitories. After moving our cases we assembled in the Dining Room for cocoa, and to meet our new companions, and Cadet Captains.

The Conway course was for six terms, and you did the first two in the Shore Base. There were 53 'New Chums' in our intake, one of the largest ever. We were divided into 5 'Tops', namely: Forecastle, Foretop, Main, Mizzen and Hold. You were then subdivided into Port and Starboard watches. Starboard Main was my allocation, and I was the second youngest of the intake. Maximum age 16. You usually kept your 'Top' throughout your training. This helped with team spirit and companionship. All very nautical. The Ship had been established for over 100 years, and some of the practices hadn't changed much.

Cadet Captains were the equivalent to prefects, except that they had much more power, including physical punishment. Thankfully most of them did not abuse this, although one or two were known to be power mad. The Junior Cadet Captain was responsible for supervising, training, and the discipline of his team. The Senior Cadet Captains would supervise two Juniors, and usually had other responsibilities as well. In overall charge of these would be the Chief Cadet Captain, or CCC. He was very important, and reported direct to the Capt Superintendent and other Senior Officers.

Discipline was administered through example, instruction, threat, fear, and as a last resort, the 'Teaser'. This was a length of thin rope, tightly spliced around a thin piece of wire, soaked in water to establish hardness, and tightness, and applied forcibly to the buttocks. Usually one or two strokes, but with a maximum of 5. The punishment would be recorded, and if blood was drawn, it had to be reported. This was frowned upon. One tended to avoid repetition.

The staff were divided into nautical and teaching, with Lieut. Commander John Brooke Smith in overall charge of the Shore Base. He was responsible for the running and discipline of the operation. He was very strict, almost old fashioned, but considered to be fair, and was highly respected. His ability to appear suddenly, without warning, earnt him the nickname of 'Spooky'.

The Shore Base had taken over half of the Marquis of Anglesey's house. The dormitories were on the first and second floors. A top would be allocated to each, and there were a dozen or so tiered bunks and narrow wardrobes around the edge. They looked smart, were fairly new, and of course we had to clean them.

The ground floor had the Dining Room, which also doubled for Assemblies and Divisions. The Entrance Hall, where the Tannoy station was established in a small office, and where the Duty Officer and Cadet would prowl. This led out into a courtyard which led up to the Kelvin Block and sports fields.

The day would start with a bosun's whistle call on the Tannoy at 0700. Quick change into running shorts and singlets, and assemble in the Courtyard. When everybody was there, and this usually took a few minutes, irrespective of weather conditions, you would then set off on a run. This was pure torture, made worse with the Duty Officers in great coats, hip flasks poking out of pockets, and steaming mugs of coffee clutched tightly in their gloved hands. No 'Amnesty International' then. This would be followed by a quick shave and breakfast. The accommodation would then be cleaned before morning Divisions. This involved lining up in 'Tops', some marching and drill, cadet inspection, short prayer and Bible reading, any instructions. Mail distribution.

Classes would then start. These were usually in the Kelvin Block, which had been converted from stables. There was also a gym. Outdoor Divisions and Parades would be held outside on the front.

Classes included Maths, Latin, Geography, History, English, Spanish, Scripture, Science, to begin with, but nautical subjects such as Navigation, Seamanship, Signals, Meteorology, Engineering and Ship Construction were introduced as the course went on. There was also prep. on most evenings.

Because of the size of the intake, we were split into 3 streams. I was put into the top one. However, I struggled to keep up with the older boys, and found myself in the relegation zone. Some boys dropped out after the first term, so we reverted to the normal 2 streams, and I was demoted into the lower one. This set a pattern, and I was moved up and down each term. On reflection I think that this was unsettling to me. I never really got to know my class mates, and as one stream was faster than the other, I think that I may have missed out on parts of the curriculum, or some sections had been rushed through. My exam results were always mid table. My opinion of the education has always been low. Thankfully Blue Funnel had an excellent training and correspondence course.

There was a lot of emphasis on practical work such as drill, marching, seamanship, rowing, sailing, boat work, and signals.

Plas Newydd from a cutter

Me in summer uniform

Lessons were also allocated to these activities.

Saturday mornings were devoted to 'clean ship'. Every cadet and 'Top' had areas of responsibility, and everything, and everywhere, was thoroughly cleaned, scrubbed, or polished for the Captain's Inspection on Sunday, irrespective of weather, or any other interruption.

Saturday afternoons were for sport. Athletics, long distance running, some cricket, sailing on the Menai Straits, limited mountaineering, but Conway was a rugby playing school. That was the most important activity, and the standards were high. Although we played against different age groups and organisations, we usually did well. A few old boys went on to representative honours at International level.

Because of my age I found myself in the Colts. The under 16s. Usually I was fly half or a three-quarter. However, there were older and bigger boys there, so I was usually second string, but when Mike Holinrake joined as scrum half, we did have a lot of fun trying to disrupt the first choices.

Sundays were the Captain's Inspection. These were very thorough and critical. They were anticipated with fear and trepidation. However, this is what happens on ships, and it means that there is always a standard of hygiene and cleanliness. It is a pity that hospitals and hotels don't follow suit, as it is very easy for basic standards to slip.

The whole Shore Base would then proceed to the Ship. This involved marching in Tops, to the dock, over half a mile away. The route went up a hill to begin with, and then had quite a steep descent. It was totally exposed to any weather. We were in our best 'Reefers' uniform, and very concerned about our appearance for the Divisions. There was a shuttle of the three motor boats to the ship, again totally exposed, but with the addition of any spray if it was at all choppy. Then there were the seagulls, which would dive bomb us with great accuracy. It was said that they were the souls of old departed Conways. No comment.

It was always a thrill to go on board the ship. This stately wooden wall, oozing history and presence. Divisions involved the whole ship's company. We would all be lined up in Tops, and inspected by the Captain and his team. A gaggle of Duty Officers, CCC, Senior Cadet Captains. Some had notebooks, all had special eye glasses that could detect a grain of salt at ten paces. They missed nothing, and wanted to impress. There was the bulge of teasers in some pockets. It was a fraught time.

When this was completed, all the Tops would march smartly up to the Main deck for the Sunday service. Traditional Matins, usually led by the Chaplain, with an occasional guest preacher. This would conclude with singing the Conway Song.

The altar and Chaplain would be in a special designated area in the middle of the ship, near to the main mast. It was known as the 'Holy Ground', and was scrubbed white, and was immaculate. Nobody dared venture on it until after the service. It was looked after by the Main Top, and it was my duty for the last two terms before the ship was lost.

Afterwards there was some free time, and we could wander around the top deck. This was always fascinating. The rigging, the views, the situation in the middle of the straits, with the occasional coaster or yacht going past. We could usually see Snowdonia in the distance.

The Shore Base would then return for lunch, and there was free time in the afternoon. Leisure activities, wander around, relax, letter writing, or visit the canteen. This was based at the far end of the main sportsfield. Available would be some basic hot snacks, tea, coffee, sweets, occasional sandwich, ice cream, and fizzy drinks. Cash was discouraged, and currency would be in books of 5 1/- vouchers, which we had drawn out. It was run by Taffy Walters, who was married to the Shore Base Nursing Sister. He would often help her out with the medical clinics, and foot rot parade.

In your third term you would join the ship. Life would be

very different, but you were now well into the course, and much more confident. The routine was now dominated by the boats. They were the only means of transport or communication with the shore. No phones, no satellites, no mobiles. There were the regular crews, supplemented by classes and duty rotas.

The three motor boats were the most popular, and each would have a Cox, who was in overall charge, including the manoeuvring. The Engineer would operate the engine controls, whilst the Bow and Stern man would attend to the ropes, and hold the boat alongside as necessary.

There was also the Water Boat, purpose built to keep the ship's tanks topped up. Rather clumsy and slow, but very effective. She would make at least two trips a day to Port Dinorwic, a small village with a small slipway towards Caernarfon. She had a regular crew, but practical classes would man her during the day. This was a popular assignment, as once she was connected up to fill, there was time to visit shops, wander around, or for those inclined, to have a smoke. This was strictly forbidden on the ship. For myself, this never interested me, although it was a big dare and challenge to some of my colleagues. My experience was, that everybody that I knew who smoked, including my Father, wanted to give up, but never could. So why start.

The Cutters were heavy, wooden, clinker built, ex naval craft, with 12 oars. Despite looking clumsy, they were actually very seaworthy and manoeuvrable. However, they had limited space for passengers or goods. The Cox would steer and give the orders to the rowers. These would be split into two rows side by side. Positions would be dictated by size, strength and experience; however we were all tried in each position. The Stroke, the oar nearest to the Cox, would regulate the stroke speed. The rest would follow. The bowman would look after the bow rope. When the order was given to toss oars, you raised your oar vertically as quickly as possible, and held it there, with the blade in a fore and aft position. The oars were of course wet,

Simpson, Orr and Brown

you got splashed, and the water ran down the pole on to your hands. It was always cold, and so were your hands. No gloves, nor do I recall any life jackets. They would have been too clumsy and awkward anyway. I can't remember any drownings or injuries. However, the chosen Heavy Weather crew did wear them. We did a lot of rowing, which I usually enjoyed, and I am certain this helped with our general fitness and strength.

The Cutters and two motor boats were hoisted out of the water every night. This involved the whole crew. The duty Top would lay out the two sets of ropes and tackles. One for the bow, and the other for the stern. We would divide equally on to these, and on orders, heave away. It was very carefully managed, but it was heavy work, and we had to be very careful not to slip, and to pull others down. The Pinnace would be hauled out to the end of a boom which protruded out near the bow, and away from damage through bumping the gangway all night. The boom was accessed by walking, or edging your way out, holding on to a wire that had been suspended above it. The boom was nearly always wet through spray or rain, and covered in seagull droppings. A bit slippery, but I do not recall any bad accidents.

At night we slept in hammocks. Metal brackets would be swung down from the deck head, a heavy beam, about 6' x 6' would be inserted and about 6 hammocks suspended on each side. They were very comfortable, this was your home. Senior cadets were allowed to use a wooden spreader, which made them even better. The last post would be played on the bugle at 2200, and it was lights out. There would be a sailor and duty officer on watch during the night. At 0530 the whole ship would wake when the diesel generators and boilers started up. Reveille would sound on the bugle at 0700. Time to lash up and stow, wash, shave, dress, and clean up for breakfast. Floppy hammocks were frowned upon, and usually punishable with 1 cut of the teaser. The washing facilities, or heads as they were known, were very basic and situated at the forward end of the deck, and were very draughty. A row of basins, the water was cold and rarely tepid, and emptied into a common open channel underneath. The toilet pans had a similar arrangement, and it had been known to float a lighted paper boat through; it certainly stopped any lingering. Baths were rationed to two a week, but showers after sport ashore helped.

The heating was very rudimentary and optimistic. However, 3 foot wooden outer walls helped with the insulation. There were always draughts.

Maintop was responsible for the rigging and sorting out of the classrooms and mess area on the main deck. This involved lowering or raising hinged panels from the deckheads, securing them, then arranging the benches and tables as required. This would be done each time.

Cadets were allocated to a mess table in Tops. There would be a Cadet Captain on each, and duties were shared, usually on a seniority basis. Sadly the food was not good, and there were two food strikes whilst I was there. The first, when I was still ashore, involved the ship only, but we all sympathised, but didn't know about it until afterwards. The second was when we were in the tents, and was organised by some of the Senior Cadet Captains. Everybody was lined up in Tops on the parade ground, and a petition was handed to the Duty Officer. It was considered, there was apprehension, after all, the ring leaders could have been expelled. Perhaps the fact that they were very important to the 1st XV was taken into consideration. However there wasn't much improvement afterwards, but there were crates of milk which we were encouraged to use.

The rigging was always a lure, and everybody was expected to go up and over the top, but under supervision. Most people enjoyed the challenge, and the first bit up to Cross Trees was quite easy, however, the next bit, over the Futtocks was frightening at first. At the top of the lower mast was a platform. This was where the top mast was joined on. The bottom of its rigging was secured to the lower mast and passed over the ends of the platform and up to the top. The bottom bit formed a 45° protrusion before resuming its normal ascent. This meant that you were climbing out and away from the mast, and had at least 10 feet to go. Gravity took an interest, so one had to be very careful, and take some time. The rigging up the top mast was fairly easy, and the next cross trees were not as wide, so this was a bit easier. The rigging up the Upper Mast was much narrower, and petered out about 6 feet from the top of the mast, which was topped off with the truck, a plate of wood about 10 inches in diameter. You could cling on to the mast and clamber up to look at and touch this feature, which many of us did. A few idiots did actually sit on the truck. This was not encouraged. Going down the other side of the rigging was considered as going over the top, and clambering down over the futtocks was not as bad, although initially you were hanging in mid-air. The Captain would sometimes greet you at the bottom. Happy to see us, or was it relief?

There was much excitement in July 1952 when HMCS *Crescent*, a destroyer, arranged to visit the ship for a few days. The Commander was an OC. She anchored a few cables away, and there were reciprocal visits, and even a gig race. This they duly won, but only just; the difference between adults and teenagers. On her departure, it was said that her crew forward were able to grab some branches off some trees when she was being turned round. It was a very tight piece of manoeuvring.

The ship's motto was 'QUIT YE LIKE MEN BE STRONG'. This always struck me as being a bit harsh and abrupt. The Petty Officers couldn't explain it, or where it came from. It is only in recent years that the full text was explained to me: *'acquit yourselves like men, be strong in the faith'*. That makes sense, and is taken from Corinthians.

We would pass under the ship's figurehead almost on a daily basis. It was very weather beaten and grubby. We would ask, *'who is it?'*, and again the POs couldn't answer. It is of course ADMIRAL NELSON, and has now been cleaned up, and stands proudly at the gate of the RN shorebase HMS *Mercury* in Portsmouth. (For a brief history of HMS *Conway*, see page 222).

The King died suddenly, early in February 1952. It was my first term on the ship.

It was a dull bleak winter, and the mood in the country was sombre. He was much loved and respected, and his leadership and activities during the war were still in recent memory. His daughter and new husband were recalled from a holiday in Kenya. Twelve months National mourning was announced. We were all issued with black arm bands. I still have mine.

The high streets, buildings, transport still showed wear from the war years. Rationing was still in force, but was gradually being eased, and there were signs of more choice in the shops. There was industrial unrest.

Gradually thoughts turned to the new era, and the Coronation next year. Conway was asked to supply two parties, and lists for volunteers duly appeared. The first party of about 40 would line up, in a prestigious position, on the procession route near to the Abbey. The second group of about 100, would help to man three warships. The cruiser H.M.S *Dido*, and destroyers, H.M.S *Camperdown*, and *Trafalgar*. I opted for the Review, and most people were selected for what they had asked for.

There were letters to parents requesting permission to go, possibly a request for donations to help pay for the extra costs, and then lists for wearing apparel to be taken appeared.

In my case, there had also been letters to shipping companies, an interview, and eventually acceptance to join Alfred Holt & Co., affectionately known as Blue Funnel. I had also applied to Union Castle who traded around Africa, but was rejected without interview because of my anticipated educational prowess. They only took 2 Cadets a year. They were probably right. Blue Funnel was a bit of a joke on Conway, as they tended to take on any of us. How wrong we were. Blue Funnel set very high standards, had a superb training programme and were considered to be a cut above the rest.

My time at Conway should have finished at Easter, but because of my age, I was told to do another term. A full 2 year Conway course entitled you to twelve months remission from the normal 4 year apprenticeship. This concession was highly prized, but you could not sit for the 2nd Mates certificate before age 20.

The Easter holiday was extended by a week, as the ship was going to be moved to Liverpool for a long overdue Dry Docking. Unfortunately there was a problem. On April 14th, whilst traversing between the bridges, she ran aground and was declared a wreck. This was a big shock, and everybody was saddened. Whatever one thought of the training, we all loved the ship. The term start was delayed, and then we were put into tents on the upper rugby pitches. It was not too bad a summer, but there was rain, and some tents leaked badly, including ours. We were moved into classrooms.

Preparations for the two groups continued, and the London crowd duly set off to do their bit.

On Monday 1st June a number of the senior cadets were invited to a Coronation Dance at the Bangor High School. This was a first, and for once dancers exceeded chaperones. There was a select dance group on the ship, but the ratio was usually 1 to 1. Usual thing, girls chattering in groups down one side of the hall, and lads nattering opposite. Eventually the ice broke, and a great evening was had by all. Some friendships developed, and a number of us met up next day, which was Coronation Day. The ship had a day off, and the cadets were dumped in Bangor, probably to allow the staff to watch the Royal proceedings. All the shops were closed, apart from a couple of kiosks. It was sunny, and we all had a very pleasant time. In those days one tended to respect new acquaintances when you first met.

Memoirs of Coronation Review Spithead

15 JUNE 1953

Reveille was at 0545 on Thursday 4th June. We caught the 0820 from Bangor, and eventually arrived at Portsmouth in the early evening. We were bussed to the dockside and ferried to the *Dido*, which was moored to buoys in the harbour. Crews were reallocated, and I stayed on *Dido*. Originally we were to man 3 destroyers. The others went off. We were taken to our mess, cocoa provided, and we settled down. We were tired and glad to sling hammocks. It was very crowded. The CPO in charge of us wasn't quite sure what to expect. Were we innocent, inexperienced, enthusiastic boys or what? We soon put him right, and I think he found us to be a bit of a handful. We were quite at home and capable of doing whatever was asked. The *Dido* was a light cruiser built by Cammel Laird in Birkenhead circa 1940. She was fast, and had 5 turrets of 5.2" guns, and had had a busy war. She was now mothballed, and in need of some TLC. A generator had been put on deck to provide the electric power. However, she was now designated the Flagship of the Reserve Fleet for the Review.

HMS Surprise, Royal review vessel

*HMS Dido mothballed,
pom-pom gun*

18

The next few days were very busy cleaning up and getting her shipshape. We also started on preparations, such as arranging wires for the lights when we dressed and illuminated the ship. There were Sunday Divisions, and we were allowed ashore for some leave in Southsea, but it was very quiet.

On Monday the ship was moved to a mooring buoy in the Solent. This was done by 2 paddle steamer tugs. They struck me as being a bit antique. However, I had been selected to be 'Commanders Doggy'. This is a very prestigious duty, and meant that I had to stand behind, and close to the Commander on formal occasions such as Divisions. My job was to carry important items such as binoculars, telescopes, documents, gloves, caps, and coats as appropriate, and to pass to, or receive these from him as needed. A sort of walking desk.

The position had big advantages. For a start I was on the Bridge when we were being towed out, lovely view, nice photo of the Review Vessel, HMS *Surprise*. Be available, keep out of the way, relaxed, no standing in a howling gale on a gun deck. It also meant that I could pull faces at my companions during these duty occasions. Such joy for a 16 year old.

The weather was generally fine and sunny, and we continued with our preparations. We also took turns to be Cadet of Watch on the Signal Bridge, or on the Quarter Deck.

On Tuesday afternoon the *Dido* contingent was taken to the two destroyers *Jutland* and *Trafalgar* for the night, and I was on the latter. The mess was a lot smaller and more congested. We wondered, just how did those sailors live, in these conditions, for months on end, and in all conditions. The two ships set off half way round the Isle of Wight and anchored off the Needles. We had no specific duties, and just assisted our colleagues generally, including preparations for dressing the ship. Next morning we joined up with the Flotilla and sailed majestically into the Solent. We were then shipped back to the *Dido*, and in the afternoon went ashore to play our hosts from the *Trafalgar* xasNAVALs REVIEW.

Cadets selecteded to attend the Naval Review are to ensure
that they are in possession of the followings of clothing Packet or otherwise.

> Monkey Jacket and trousers.
> Cap.and cap covers.
> White shirts.
> Stiff collars.
> Blue shirts.
> Soft collars.
> Lanyards.
> Two pairs of Blue shorts.
> Black stockings.
> Garters.
> Black socks.
> Handerchiefs.
> Pyjamas
> Uniform shoes. (Best and working no toecaps.)
> Boot cleaning material.
> Oilskin. and Sea boots.
> Raincoat.
> Gloves uniform
> Clothes mending gear.
> Fortnights underwear.
> Two towels.
> Overalls.
> Toilet gear.
> Clothes brush.
> Hair brush.
> Sheets and pillow cases.
> Suit cases (No kit bags allowed.)
In addition it is advisable to take a blue pull over and a
hite sweater.

ptional gear. Sports gear.
Slippers or gym shoes.

Don Bell
in summer uniform

REMEMBER

1. Always salute the Q.D. when passing or crossing it and when coming onboard.
2. The correct reply to an order is "AYE, AYE SIR" and not O.K. or Right Ho.
3. All bugle calls and/or pipes are to be obeyed at the double.
4. The Naval custom of no talking after "Pipe Down" is to be carried out.
5. When given the order "Dismiss," always turn Right or Forward, dwell a pause and break off. Do NOT salute.
6. When on shore you are to salute Officers at all times. Whilst onboard ship it is not necessary to salute an Officer when passing, but you should do so if he speaks to you. As a mark of respect you should stand smartly to attention when passed by an Officer onboard ship. Do NOT salute when not wearing a cap, but stand to attention.
7. If you are 16 years of age or over you may purchase 100 Duty Free Cigarettes during your week's stay onboard. You are NOT allowed to take more than 25 of these cigarettes ashore with you at any one time, which includes the day of leaving the ship.
NOTE.—These cigarettes are for your own PERSONAL use and must not be given or SOLD to any other person whatsoever.
If you do NOT smoke DO NOT BUY ANY CIGARETTES, then you will avoid getting into trouble.

at cricket. We of course won, and I had a good day. Took 3 wickets, and then scored 30 not out. A happy fellow. We did have some free time afterwards.

On Wednesday we were taken on a Motor Fishing Vessel (MFV), and went round the assembled fleet. Probably one of the largest collections of warships ever, with vessels of all sorts of shapes and sizes from all over the world. The Russians sent a destroyer and the cruiser *Sverdlov*. She created a lot of interest, as she was very new, and hadn't been seen before and probably the most destructive vessel present. Whilst we were there, there were rumours that the headless body of a frogman had been found. This was hushed up, and years later we found out that it was probably Commander Buster Crabbe, an old Conway. There were also rumours that he had been captured, and then set up in the Soviet Union. These were tense times with the cold war building up. The excursion was a terrific experience, and I was able to take a number of photos.

Back on board we continued with preparations to dress the ship, set up the lights for illuminations, Cheer Ship practices, and general cleaning, including the torpedo tubes. On Sunday there were Divisions, and my new found position came into its own.

Don Bell and I joined at the same time, and were actually the two youngest in our term. We were allocated to the same Top, Starboard Main, and we always got on very well. He also joined Blue Funnel, but we soon lost contact. He is in our summer day uniform. Blue shirts and shorts.

Monday was Review Day. It was fine, cloudy and the visibility was good.

We were able to listen to the Marine Band on the Quarter Deck, always a great experience.

H.M.S *Surprise* left her berth at 1500, and when she approached the lines, the Fleet fired the Royal Salute. What an experience to be in the middle of. My position was on the Bridge with the Commander and the Senior Officers, Admirals, official guests, and that sort of thing. The Captain's Doggy and I kept to the back of the proceedings, and had a wonderful view, and were able to use our boss's binoculars. VIPs of course.

Our colleagues were not so lucky. They were lined up next to the signal gun on turret platform 3. They were told that there would be some bangs, all 21 of them. These guns are designed to be heard at three miles, and in all conditions. The first shot came as a great shock, and caused much disturbance in the ranks. As did the rest. There were no ear muffs, nor any other attempt to deaden the sound. Unfortunately, a photographer from a well known magazine was present, and duly took his photos of the distress. Probably tipped off where to be. When we saw these in the next edition, we were not amused, and we all cancelled our orders. We had done our best to co-operate and to do a good job, we felt let down. It was not a battle situation. That magazine closed down a few years later. No tears were shed.

At 1640 we went to our positions, and I was back on the Bridge. As the *Surprise* went by, we cheered ship. This involved caps off, and on the instruction, three circular movements of the arm. She anchored not far away. There was then the Fly Past.

Guests then departed, and the fleet was illuminated at 2030 until 2359. There was a fireworks display. This was all very impressive. Two ships lit up early, accidentally of course. Give you one guess which one of them was.

The *Surprise* left on Tuesday to a 21 gun salute. The order had been issued 'splice the main brace'. This was anticipated, but welcomed all the same. This is the Monarch's traditional extra tot of rum issued to all hands, as a thank you, but not Conway Cadets. We were displeased, but the regular sailors reluctantly had to drink our portions. At 1600 the ship was towed back into the harbour and alongside H.M.S *Jamaica*.

Reveille at 0500, train back to Bangor, arrived 1945. Back to Conway routine. It was end of my last term. There were exams, boat duties, including going in the pinnace to the ship wreck, to set up a paraffin lamp to mark a shipping hazard. This was a daily routine. There were vaccinations, correspondence to new employers, and a rocket to all hands from the Captain Superintendent about getting involved with girlfriends.

The Queen did a tour of the country, mostly by train, and this included North Wales and Caernarvon. On her way back she was to drive through Port Dinorwic. It was arranged that the ship's company would line up, and that the cavalcade would slow down. However, some of us had had vaccinations, and were on sick leave. So we were allowed to go to the High Street, and were actually very close to the cars. We were in uniform, and the Queen acknowledged our salutes. One of the locals nearby kindly sent me the enclosed photo, which was taken over our shoulders.

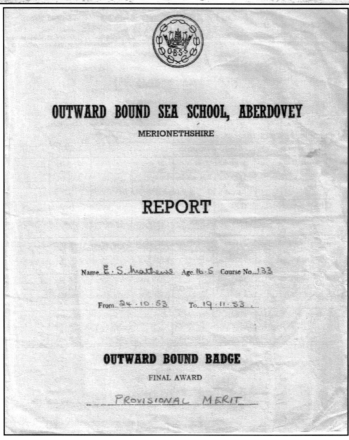

Memoirs of the Outward Bound Sea School, Aberdovey

OCTOBER 1953

The Outward Bound Sea School, or Aberdovey as we shortened it to, was held in awe and respect by Conway Cadets. Tales of 0500 reveilles, early morning runs, cold showers, treks into the mist and distant mountains, and impossible projects, had all been lovingly embellished.

The school was run by a Trust, and was designed to foster fellowship, team spirit, and to cope with challenges that one hadn't faced before. It was all about character building. The courses ran for 3 to 4 weeks, and were under the supervision of Capt Fuller, a famous Olympic oarsman.

Many shipping companies insisted that their cadets attended, including Blue Funnel, despite 2 years at Conway. We had to pay. A number of employers also sent budding trainees for some practical and challenging experiences. As did some local Authorities with troublesome and repetitive miscreants. In my case I had left Conway at the end of July, but because of my age, was not to be appointed until December. So a course in October was fine, although perhaps it was a chilly time of the year to be going off to Cardigan Bay. There was another Conway on the course, we knew each other and were good friends.

My journey took me through London on to Paddington and then up to Shrewsbury. It was a dull grey drizzly afternoon. The platform was very busy, and when the train drew in we were smothered in steam.

We had to make sure that we were in the right half, as when the train reached Machynllech, it would separate, one part going south to Aberystwyth and the rest up to Aberdovey and beyond. The carriages were antique. No corridor, no ventilation, and poor lighting. A bunch of strangers, and nothing to see.

We arrived at Penhelig Halt about 1745. This was a small platform built for the school, and by now it was very dark. We disembarked and were told to leave our luggage at the roadside and proceed up a winding, steep, and dark driveway to the school. After a while we became aware of a dim glow in the distance, and we were soon into a large lit room. Instructions, hut allocations, collect uniform, take cases to the huts, and then return for medicals, interviews and eventually some supper. 2200 turn in.

We were all very tired, and it was a cold night. No heating.

On Sunday reveille was at 0630, and we all got on with getting up, washing, and pre-breakfast duties. Breakfast at 0830, and then more interviews and medicals finished off.

In the afternoon there was a parade, we were introduced to the staff and there was a half hour drill. The hut Captains and Vice Captains were announced, and reallocation of teams took place. There was a short talk on map reading, which was followed by a walk over the nearby hill to a friendly farm. We trotted back. In the evening there was a lecture and discussion on the idea and principle of the OBS School.

Reveille on Monday was at 0700. Into shorts, and go for a run. Topped up with a cold shower. The supervisors were of course wrapped up, and they made sure that everybody got well under and were well soaked. Actually, after a short while it wasn't too bad. Pre-breakfast duties included cleaning up the huts and surrounds, and taking the 'pig swill' bins to the farm.

There was an inspection of the dormitories, a parade, and then we marched to the wharf in Aberdovey. Here we did some storing and maintenance of the boats. We were marched back for lunch, and then to the wharf again for boat handling and rowing in the afternoon. This was closed with our first boat drill, where we had to lift and swing out one of the cutters. We did quite well, and were driven back to the school. In the evening we had a pleasant church service, and then we were given the 'training conditions' and joined in a swearing in ceremony. The routine was now beginning to be established.

There were courses, lectures and practical sessions on map reading, first aid, artificial respiration, (the Schaeffer Method), sailing and tacking, lifeboat instruction, rowing, ropes and knots.

Groups were assigned to support the local lifeboat, coastguard and mountain rescue teams. The lifeboat team was called out once. There were some very interesting talks. Exciting stuff.

Some of these took place in the evenings, as did some of the church services. This was a new experience for some of the students, but I felt that most were happy with the occasion.

There was an evening of Sea Shanties led by Mr Hugeot, one of the Petty Officers. He was much older than the rest of the staff, and had served in sailing ships. There were not many active survivors of that age. He had a national reputation, and it was a thoroughly enjoyable time. The school encouraged and helped him to write some historical books. Recently I visited the 2008 Tall Ships gathering in Liverpool. There was a music group singing shanties in one of the marquees. When I spoke to them after they had finished, it turned out that they were fans of Mr Hugeot, and had been inspired by him.

There was an ongoing athletics programme which we all had to join in and complete. We were all timed and measured as appropriate, and compared to some basic standards. Any improvements were duly noted. It wasn't too onerous, and gave you the opportunity to try activities that may have passed you by previously - in my case shot and discus.

There was a commando assault course. We were allowed to try this, but then we were shown how to do it properly and put through a very vigorous test. Great stuff.

There were some expeditions. These included a trek to the Hostile Farm, reputedly not a fan of the school. However they seemed OK to us.

There was an all day trek to, and up, Cader Idris. We set off on bikes at 1000 through Towyn then Birds Rock to a NCU café. Cup of tea and some cake, and we started to climb. We soon stiffened up and it became quite hard work. At the top it was cloudy and very cold, we had our sandwiches, but there were glimpses of some lovely views. We took a different route back down to a lake. It was more of a scramble and slither over loose slate chippings. We arrived at the café at 1600, more tea and cake, then back to the School. It was a quiet evening, and we were all glad of an early turn in. A thoroughly enjoyable and satisfying day.

Guy Fawkes was duly remembered with a big bonfire, and impressive firework display. We all had 4 days on the *Warspite*, a sailing ketch - two masts and big sails. She was anchored outside of the estuary bar. The weather had deterioted and the sea was lively. We upped anchor and set sail for Abersoch, a few hours away. We were all very seasick, but some recovered quicker than others, including myself, so we ended up doing the various duties of steering, clearing up and look out.

We anchored off the lifeboat house, and the Captain wanted a trip ashore. This was in a skiff, a small rowing boat, and I was in the crew. The weather had moderated a little, the *Warspite*'s movements eased, but it was still cloudy and windy. It was good to have a wander ashore, and he duly had his pint - sorry, attended to Master's business. Anchor watches were started with two on each watch for two hours. This meant checking that we weren't dragging our anchor, by taking compass bearings, and keeping alert.

Next day we all scrubbed the decks and cleaned up generally. We were given some basic navigation instruction and shown our position on the chart; there were sessions of rope knots and splicing. The food was excellent, but we did have to peel the spuds. We had to change our anchorage position.

On the last day, reveille was at 0300, and we all hauled up the anchor by hand, and set sail back to Aberdovey. We of course handled the sails. There was rain about. We had to wait for the tide at the bar, but were soon alongside and back to the school. A very enjoyable experience.

A few days later there was another expedition. The big one, the one that we had all been apprehensively training for. Reveille 0500, morning run and cold shower. 0615, breakfast and then parade. We were divided into parties, and bussed to Barmouth Junction. We were given maps and compasses, and different routes. We all set off and were soon into cloud. We found some map positions, but were soon lost. There were very few distinctive marks, and you couldn't see them anyway. However with brilliant map skills, sheer luck, and perhaps a little help from a couple of farmers that we came across, we arrived at our check point. Here we were met, had a map reading test, some lunch, and then off again. We were the second group to report in. We had to change our intended route because of some floods. We were soon in cloud again, and got lost again. Eventually we found our way back to base. A hot bath and huge relief. We had done it. We had covered over 35 miles.

Much time was spent doing boat work. Early in the course when in the cutter, I had usually sat in the stroke position, so that I could quietly pass help to the Duty Cox. Conway experience was very useful. After a while the instructors cottoned on to this, and pushed me further away. By this time most people had started to get the hang of things. There was the ongoing lifeboat drill. We were assigned to teams, and each person allocated a duty, which we took turns to do. The most important job was no: 6. Whilst the team lifted the boat out of its cradle and held it there, he had to secure the rope fall to the crucifix bollard with 6 turns of the rope, as quickly as possible. The boat would then be swung out and set for the lowering position. The whole operation would be timed. Because of my Conway experience I was quite quick at this, and it became my job in the team. Early on the teams would take over two minutes. We won the competition with 54 seconds. No prizes, but a nice compliment.

Whilst we were on the course, the P & O Steamship company donated an aluminium lifeboat the "Awatea". Between us we had stored, rigged and set it up. Lifeboats are designed to float and stand up to robust conditions. They are not very manoeuvrable, and when light are very high out of the water. This makes rowing difficult. There was to be a handing over ceremony, and I was in the crew. We had to row the boat from moorings in the river to the slip, there was a speech by Lord Burghley, three cheers, row around the wharf and then back to the moorings. Joy and happiness all round.

The Bishop of Bangor came down to dedicate a Memorial Window in the Chapel. The course duly closed. Most of us had thoroughly enjoyed it, and made some good friends. It was noticeable, that many of those that had joined with an attitude problem, and a reputation, had become very enthusiastic and keen members of the course. It was great to be with them. A terrific experience.

So, back to civilisation. A long tedious journey. On the way home I had time to break it and call in on my old school Beaumont House near Chorleywood. They gave me a very big welcome, and were very interested in my Conway and OBSS experiences.

Midshipman

Dec 1953 - Apr 1957

The letter arrived. 'We have appointed you to our M.V. *Ascanius* etc etc'. Much excitement and scurrying around. Preparations. My first voyage. It was the only time that we had a letter from the company with joining instructions. From now on it would be a curt reply paid telegram. When you left a ship you took all your gear with you. You would be given a rough idea of how many days leave you could expect, but nothing else. 'Report to India Buildings at 0900 on Monday xyz with your deep sea gear'. Acknowledge'. No indication of ship, length of voyage, or where you would be going. You simply had to take everything with you, including your sextant. We always travelled in uniform. This went back to war years, when young males, usually MN, who were not in uniform had been beaten up. The fact that some of them had been through hell to get food onto the tables, supplies for the forces to keep going, and to bring loved ones home in one piece, was usually ignored. What a grateful society.

To begin with you would travel up on the Sunday to Holm

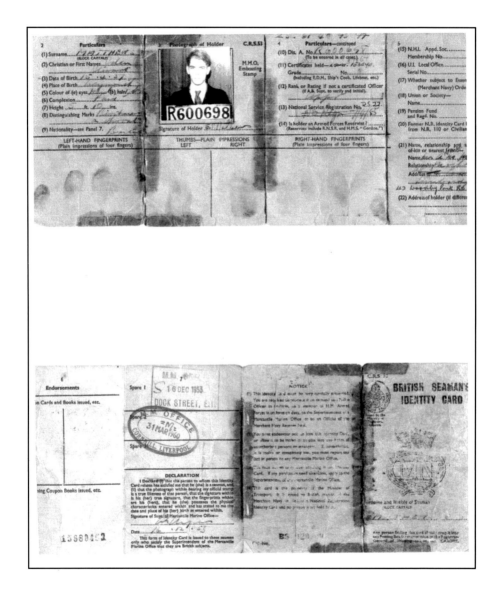

Lea, the company hostel for Middies. Heavy cases would be deposited in the Left Luggage Office at Lime Street station. The hostel was run by two ladies, who were both widows of Chief Stewards who had perished during the war. The company had a reputation for trying to do the right thing. They were very efficient and business like. It cannot have been easy to cope with an ever changing bunch of excitable but very worldly teenagers. Having said that, there was an occasion when I had to stay over for a weekend when everybody else had left. Saturday was Cup Final day, and I was invited to join them to visit a neighbour who had a television. Black and white of course, and Sunderland won. A big shock. Being 'Scouseland', I was treated as a member of the family. Much appreciated.

All Cadets had to sign 4 year Indentures. These set out the conditions of our employment and were very rigid. They were also strictly enforced. Conway Cadets had 12 month remission, but in my case, because of my age, it was only 9 months. Rates of pay were set out. £7.50/m for the first 3 months. Then £9.50/m for the next 12, then £11.00/m, and finally £12.00/m. Out of this you had to provide your own clothes, uniforms, text books, sextant and instruments, personal expenses. Also extra expenses when travelling, although a rail voucher was provided. There was no allowance for inflation.

After a couple of years I was given the tip off to travel overnight on the Sunday, arrive 0500, deposit the cases, offer 2/6 (half a crown) to the night porter, and have a couple of hours kip on a settee in the very grand lounge of the Adelphi Hotel. There were other bodies scattered around. A visit to the luxurious cloakroom downstairs. A wash, shave, change and spruce up, would be followed by a full English breakfast, no room numbers requested, and saunter off to the office fully refreshed. Very civilised, and also meant that you gained almost another day at home. This was very precious. At the time, the Adelphi was the prestigious and number one hotel in the North West.

The hostel was well known locally, and bus conductors would usually call it out in good time. However on one occasion one was a little too clever and called out, 'holts baby farm'. There were a number of us standing. The first took him off with us, and the last rang the bell. Next morning we were all summoned in the office and given a real dressing down. Danger, reputation, safety, review of Indentures etc. Final warning. This remained as company folk lore for years to come, and still causes much amusement.

Time in the office was usually spent on reviewing the correspondence course that you had done the previous voyage, and some instruction on the next phase. There would be individual interviews, and you would meet your next companions. First trippers would also have an interview with Mr Heathcote, the Director in charge of training. He gave the impression of being a bit Victorian, but we respected what he said, and on reflection I think that we accepted that what he said was right. We were given a letter, but he also told us that when we went ashore, that we represented Great Britain, to conduct ourselves with dignity and to respect the locals. Also to avoid the temptations of the flesh, particularly in the Far East. We were quickly aware of the dangers, and most of us observed this.

Sometimes courses would be arranged including the Lifeboat course. This was compulsory for all company seagoers. This involved instruction and rowing around Salthouse dock, now the Maritime Museum.

EDH (efficient deck hand). This was the course that the sailors had to pass before becoming established, and involved the practical work that they did, including knots, working with wires, ropes, cargo rigging, safety etc. It was company philosophy, that in our training, we could do any job that we might have to ask a sailor to do.

Radar. This was emerging technology for the MN, and BF tended to treat it with caution. However, they did establish a radar station on the top of a Gladstone dock shed, which was well used. We of course took to it happily. Senior Officers were not so keen. The accurate plotting of ships movements at sea was of course crucial, and needed instruction and practice. Not all ships had it on board.

Wire splicing experience. The company had a Rope Locker in Birkenhead. This is where mooring ropes etc were prepared and despatched to the ships. There was also a wire splicing section. This required special skills for mooring wires and lifeboat falls. We all did a week's stint. It was difficult, but very interesting.

Courses on First Aid and also VHF were also conducted on the ships.

Midshipman is a Royal Navy rank. It was conferred on Blue Funnel Cadets during the 1st World War by the King. Apparently a ship had been sunk, and all the Senior Officers had been killed. Three lifeboats got away with some passengers and crew. A 17 year old Cadet took charge, and guided the survivors to a safe landfall, 700 miles away. We were all very proud of this, and most of us after 12 months at sea could have, and would have, done the same. We were a very confident and aware lot.

After a couple of days we were told that we would be joining the ship on Wednesday, and probably sail late on Friday 23rd December. She was berthed in Vittoria dock Birkenhead, where most of our deep sea voyages would start from. The Halfdeck hadn't been used for a couple of weeks, so our first job was to open up everything, ventilate, and give a good clean up. This was to be our home for the next three months. The heavy cases were brought down from Lime Street, so we were able to settle in. There were four of us, including two first trippers. On Friday we assisted with the ship's seagoing preparations. This included making our own way, ie walk, to the Shipping Federation in

Hamilton Square. Here the whole crew would have to 'sign on', and you would meet your new shipmates. A regular question would be 'who is the Old Man' and who is the 'Mate'. These would be our Gods for the foreseeable future. Dougie Stroud was the Master. Very experienced, quiet, but could be very perceptive and sharp. Belsen Boyd was the Mate. He was a bachelor, with a reputation for being totally committed to the job, no humour, no empathy, and no patience. Short cropped hair.

On return to the ship there were stores to check and a Pre-sailing Inspection. This involved a quick tour of the ship by the Master, a Director, and the Senior Captain Superintendent. All smiles. We were allocated our stand - by duties and watches. As the cargo finished, all the hatches would be covered, and all derricks lowered and secured by the sailors and carpenter. It was blowing outside.

OUTWARD BOUND

A typical voyage based on: M.V. ASCANIUS (aka Ashcan),
my first ship.

Stand-by was at 2200, and I found myself forward, with the Mate. Full uniform, my main duty was to answer the Bridge telephone. A solid instrument in a heavy metal case, which would be stowed away when not in use. Even so, it showed signs of bad weathering, and I could not make out what the Third Officer was saying. He had a soft Scottish voice, and I of course had never done this before. Thankfully the Mate knew what was needed. Nothing was said, but I felt it had been a complete disaster. We were towed out by 2 tugs and manoeuvred into the lock basin. It took about an hour for the water levels to equalise, and next minute you were out into the Mersey, dock Pilot dropped, full ahead and away you go. You could feel the power of the engines building up, and soon the bright friendly lights of Liverpool and the low coastline would drop behind. It became very black with just the buoy lights flashing. We sailed past the Bar Lightship and Pilot cutter, where most ships dropped their Pilots, at speed, and due west to Holyhead, 6 hours away. It was blowing.

Blue Funnel ships cut inside the Skerries Island to drop the Pilot off Holyhead, and I was on duty to help a sailor with the Pilot ladder. This was made of rope with wooden steps and longer spacers, it was very heavy and difficult to manage. It was now blowing a full gale and the seas were very lively. As we manoeuvred into position, the ship rolled awkwardly and the sailor lost his grip, suddenly I found myself with the full weight of the ladder, clinging on like mad. Thankfully a wave took some of the weight off me and as the ship rolled back he was able to grab hold. The Holyhead pilot boat always looked very small to me, and I always marvelled at how the Pilots could clamber in and out of such a small, open, and very bouncy boat. We then rolled up and stowed the ladder away, the ship was manoeuvred out to sea, and Full Speed Away was rung. This is the double ring on the telegraph to tell the Engineers to build up to full seagoing revs, and to assume seagoing routines. Bardsey Island light, usually very dim, would be the last we would see of the UK for some time. The ship would start bumping into the waves. Time for bed.

Watchkeeping meant keeping a look out on the weather side of the bridge, trying to keep warm and dry, and making tea as appropriate. Most importantly, calling the next watch at one bell. This was at a quarter to the hour, and involved tapping on the side of the victim's bunk, and again at five to. Watches were split into three four hour sessions. 12-4, 4-8, 8-12. After 24 hours we came off watches. It was Christmas Day. We were now in the Bay of Biscay, and it was a full gale. Enjoy the

DINNER.

Cream of Tomato

Fried Haddock Toast, Meunière
Baked Halibut, Tartare Sauce

Asparagus, Vinaigrette

Roast Turkey, Chipolata
Braised York Ham, Spinach
Green Peas   Brussels Sprouts
Rissolée & Natural Potatoes

Plum Pudding, Brandy Sauce
Christmas Cake   Mince Pies
Strawberry Sundae

Assorted Nuts
Dessert   Coffee

M.V. "Ascanius"
Commr. R. W. Bond

CHRISTMAS DAY
1953.

Christmas 1953

M.V. "ASCANIUS" XMAS DAY 1953

A queasy Christmas

photos. The family had given me some presents, but opening these was deferred. As we moved south the weather gradually improved and soon we were off Spain. Cape Finisterre, then C. St Vincent, where we turned south east towards the Medi, and then past Gibraltar.

Day work started with a call at 0530 by the stand by sailor. The junior, or duty Middie, would start to make the tea, the others would get on with getting ready to turn to, and the senior would trot off to the bridge to see the Mate for our orders. At 0600 the junior would start on clearing and cleaning the halfdeck, whilst the others would usually go to the bridge.

The halfdeck would be washed, scrubbed, and polished, as appropriate, every day where possible. We made our own bunks.

The bridge party would sweep or scrub the deck as needed, polish the brass, clean the windows. Being in a constantly damp and salty environment, this needed doing daily.

At 0745, one bell, we would all stop, return to the halfdeck, wash, shave, shower as needed, change into full uniform, and proceed to the saloon at 0800 for a full English breakfast. This would be served by the table steward.

At 0900 we started work on deck. Our first job was with the sailors, overhauling and maintaining the cargo derricks and gear. There were 6 hatches with at least 4 derricks on each. A sailor would go to the top of a derrick post, detach the top block, which held the cargo wires, and this would be lowered to the deck. This was a very heavy and clumsy job. The block would be dismantled, cleaned, inspected and thoroughly greased. The wires would also be checked. After much use these would flatten, go soft, and a number of broken strands would appear. The wire would then be condemned and replaced. The wires would be greased thoroughly, reassembled and reinstated. There would be 2 or 3 groups working at this, but it still took a few days, and was heavy going. You were on the open deck, it would be windy, and early on, chilly. This is where I acquired

Fun and games

EDEN S. MATHEWS

my nickname, Tony. First time out, I was working with the same sailor that had been on the pilot ladder, and he asked me my name. I said 'Mathews', he said 'no no, your Christian name', I said 'Eden'. He couldn't pronounce it, it was too soft, and in the wind it was lost. So, spur of the moment, as Anthony Eden was a well known name, we quickly established an abbreviation to Tony. It has of course stuck.

Other day jobs would include helping the sailors to scrub the decks using salt water hoses, and brooms. This I found to be very tiring. Sometimes we used sand. Sujiing the paintwork on the outside of the accommodation. This involved using bare hands and cotton waste into a solution of water and soda crystals. Very good at removing encrusted salt, grease and most substances, including skin, flesh and finger nails. Not very pleasant. Washing the varnished rails with fresh water was a lot easier.

As the ship proceeded into the Medi, it became warmer and more pleasant, and the Old Man would authorize that we could go into 'whites'. Always a welcome time. We would also start to work on our own. Very often this was maintenance around the boat decks.

If ships carried more than 11 passengers, they had to have a Doctor on board. If not, then in most companies, the Chief Steward would be the Doctor. Very rarely did they have any special training. However, Blue Funnel usually carried a Male Nurse. These were hand picked and usually very interesting guys. On this voyage he often came up for a chat. His uncle was 'Pierrepoint' the last official 'hangman'. Some very interesting discussions took place. Sometimes we played Monopoly. He seemed to win regularly, and we got a bit fed up. After a while he gave us his secrets, and they worked. On another ship, the '*Troilus*', which had very long sea passages, we often played 2 – 3 games in the afternoon. I became very unpopular when I won 14 consecutive games. No secrets passed on.

41

Port Said 1955

*Port Swettenham
anchorage*

Clytonius at sea

After 9 days, we would enter Port Said and tie up to buoys to await our turn in the south bound convoy. Mail from home was always very welcome, but security was the priority. Theft was a serious problem. All windows had to be closed tight, and doors locked. There was no air conditioning, so it became very uncomfortable inside. A Middie would be stationed on the bow and poop to protect the mooring ropes. It was very hectic, but good fun. The 'Gippoes' could be very amusing. The Gily-Gily Man would mesmerise us with his sleight of hand. A small container would be suspended over the bow containing a searchlight. This would be manned by the Electrician, who would be in phone contact with the bridge. We would also lift a small mooring boat and 2 men, onto the foredeck, to handle the ropes if we needed to tie up to the bank to let the northbound convoy through. Sometimes this would happen in the Bitter Lakes where you would be at anchor. It usually took 24 hours to traverse the canal. At Port Suez you would slow down to drop off the Pilot and any shore staff, and 'orft' you go. Full speed down the Red Sea to Aden.

Aden was a bunkering port, and you would tie up to 2 mooring buoys. This was engineer's 'palava', so we just pottered about, and sorted out our mail. A barren and not a very attractive looking place. After 6 hours or so we would be ready to go, due east, full speed to Penang, 9 days away.

Day work would now be working with the sailors, mainly chipping and scraping paintwork, including the metal decks. Noisy, dusty, and very hot under the open sun. Most people wore hats and usually covered up. Sun bathing was not a sensible option. At 1030 we would all stop for a 15 minute 'smoko'. This could be tea, coffee, or lime juice. By law, all MN ships had to carry 2 demijohns of concentrated lime juice. This was to combat scurvy, and dated back to sailing ship days. On well fed ships this was not a problem, and most Chief Stewards would pass these on to the Middies. It was vile. However, mixed with

Yank a bit close

Penang

Gibralta

cold water, sugar, stirred well, it could be quite presentable and refreshing. Work would stop at 1145, one bell, and we would have to shower, change into uniform, and be ready for lunch at 1200. Restart at 1300. However chipping would be stopped so that watchkeepers could rest. The afternoon would be red leading the morning's work. Smoko at 1500, and finish at 1600. Time to clean up, rest, and possibly do some correspondence course. Maybe. Sometimes a 'zis' took over.

The passage across the Indian Ocean could be idyllic. Light breezes, very long low swell, ship moving gently. Glorious weather. Flying fish scudding away at speed, porpoises and dolphins, occasional whales, shark, turtles. Many ships would erect the portable swimming pool, and deck games would become regular features. Tennis or cricket were the most popular. The company would supply some equipment, netting, narrow bats, balls, and quoits. However these had a short lifespan, and Middies soon became adept at making rope quoits, and string cricket balls. Done properly and soaked in salt water overnight, these could be very hard and fast. Also if a seam was sown on, you could get some spin. A sloping, moving deck, and suitable obstructions could also be used to good effect. A ball that went over the side was 6 and out, irrespective of the circumstances, or rank. Dinner, usually very nice meals, at 1800. Time to study. We usually turned in at 2200. Early start.

At sea the main event would be the 'noon' sight. Senior Middies would take it in turn to join in the ceremony. After breakfast, all the Mates, including the Master, would take a morning sight of the sun to establish a longitude line. This would be calculated up to when the noon latitude sight could be taken. The 2nd Mate would try to arrange the nightly clock changes so that this was as close to noon as possible. This was the point when the sun was due south. Everybody involved would be lined up with their sextants, and avidly follow the sun to its highest point or altitude. At this the Old Man would go round everybody and select the mean reading, usually his.

Noon sight

Red Sea, 1957

Everybody would then rush to their space, and calculate where the two lines met. This would give their position. Some quicker than others. The Master and 2nd Mate (navigator), would then decide on the ship's position. This would be despatched to the Radio Officer ASAP, and he would send it on when he was on watch next, to India Buildings. Here the Directors had a daily midday meeting, where an illuminated globe with each ships noon position would be shown.

DISCHARGING

At Penang you would either anchor, or sometimes go alongside. This is where the voyage started. It is a wide river estuary, with a small dock area of up to 3 wharves. The background was of low hills. Barges would be used in which to discharge cargo. All hatches would be open and worked. There would be at least a dozen gangs on board. Work was 24/24 and 7/7. The 2nd mate would look after the after hatches, and the 3rd mate the forward ones. A Middie would be at each end, usually cargo watching. This meant being stuck down a hatch, or locker, for up to 6 hours, often without a break. Usually there would be a security man, so, you would be watching him, watching you. Sometimes you could get into a chat, but often you were too tired to bother. No ventilation, and very sticky, noisy, and dusty. The Middies would try to use normal watches, but usually it was either 6 on and 6 off, or 12 on and 12 off. If the ship sailed, or moved, or docked, in your off time, tough. We tried to relieve each other for meals. It was very demanding. Approved tradesmen would also set up their stalls on deck, and you could replace jeans, hats, toiletries etc. It was here that I bought my first sarong. By far the best wear for nights in the tropics.

Outward cargo could include: all construction materials, all sorts of vehicles, chassis to railway wagons or buses, railway engines and wagons, rails, cartons of Guinness, other beers and lagers, household stores, Nescafe, soap, bags of sea mail, wines and spirits. Valuables would be in kept special lockers.

After 2- 3 days you would sail overnight to Port Swettenham. This was a few hours up a river, surrounded by mangrove foliage, vegetation, and airless. A tropical hell hole. Most ships anchored in the wide river, and discharged into barges. But there were 2 berths for difficult cargoes. My young fertile mind always imagined the Japs coming round the corner armed to the teeth in gunboats. Having said that, I did have some very happy times there. There was a small club for seafarers run by a Padre. He would organise inter-ship football matches, and on one occasion we played cricket on Christmas Day, on a mat wicket. It was often our first run ashore for a few weeks, and it was work hard, play hard. Mail from home was now arriving regularly. The company had a system whereby letters would be posted to HO, clearly marked with ship's name and your rank. These would be bundled up and forwarded to the appropriate Agent. The Pilot would often bring it on board, for the Purser to sort out and pass on. Very welcome. Port Swettenham served mid-Malaya, rubber plantations and all that.

After 3 or 4 days, orft to Singapore, and civilisation.

A day's run, and you would usually have to anchor to wait for a berth. The roads were always busy, and there would be other company ships. The Mates or Middies would keep anchor watches, and wait for the signal station to call up by morse lamp, and give instructions.

Singapore is a fairly low and flat island, about the size of the Isle of Wight. It is completely independent of Malaya. It is surrounded by many islands of different sizes. It is where Ian Fraser, an Old Conway, had won his VC. He had guided a mini-sub, in broad daylight, submerged, into the docks. Here his crewman had placed a mine to a Jap cruiser, and despite a falling tide which was trapping them to the seabed, they made sure that it was placed properly, before trying to extricate themselves. This they did, and were duly rescued by a sub outside, 80 miles away. The cruiser was badly holed and rested on the seabed. He died recently, but had regularly attended the Conway reunions. A very modest man. The waters were very clear, and any passing plane would have seen them.

The docks area ran alongside one side of the island, opposite another, with a channel between. There was space for 30-40 ships. It would be very hot, but drier than Malaya, and more bearable. The docks worked 3 shifts. 0800-1100, 1300-1600, 1800-2100. This was living. The only days off would be at Xmas. They were enclosed, with guards on each gate, and you were issued with passes. They were safe. The citizens of Singapore had provided a property for the use of visiting seafarers. Possibly to try to keep them off the streets of their city. Connell House was well used. It had a large airy room, bar, food, table tennis, swimming pool, and was occasionally used for socials, or films. It was a very long walk from the ships, usually a taxi job if funds allowed. There was a Mission to Seaman Padre stationed there, and he would arrange soccer games against other ships, or the military. There was a small, but very nice little chapel there, and the Sunday communion service was much appreciated. Those who were interested would be collected and returned afterwards. It had been used as a rice storage facility during the War by the Japs. He would also invite those who had the time off, to share Sunday lunch with his family. He was always available to have a chat.

A visit to the city was always interesting. The shops, 'Change Alley', Bougie Street, cricket ground, and Raffles Hotel. Seafarers were not welcome there. The notorious 'Change Alley was a narrow passage with street vendors and shops closely packed. It was a pickpocket's haven, but good fun, and there were some bargains to be had. Bougie Street was internationally known for the cross dressers and transsexuals.

Tiger Balm Gardens exhibit

Hong Kong

It was a great source of amusement to us. A visit to one of the cinemas was a special treat. Tickets had to be booked, and you went in your best shore going gear. The theatre was on two levels with a large lounge area on each. It was air conditioned and had a good sized cocktail bar. Chilled Tiger lager was very popular. A buzzer was sounded 5 minutes before the start. There would be an interval, with plenty of time to replenish. Very civilised. The Tiger Balm Gardens, a Chinese Malayan outside museum, were well worth a visit. On a later voyage, a small group of us hired a car and drove across to the mainland. We were all very conscious of the Communist terrorist activities, but thankfully these did not affect us. We would often see the special armoured wagons, which would be stationed at each end of a train.

After 4 days or so it was onwards to Hong Kong, and this would take 3 to 4 days. Starts to get more windy and cooler.

What a contrast and culture shock. Hong Kong is a very hilly island and very populated surrounded by many other, but smaller ones. There was a cliff top railway to the highest point, and as you can see I did this once when on the *Demodocus*. This was its maiden voyage, and we had joined the ship in Newcastle. A very different experience, and this is where I sailed with John Hall, who later joined Cunard, and was on the QE 2 to the Falklands, and later became Staff Captain. The island is very built up with many skyscrapers. On the way in, a Military cemetery was pointed out to me on the side of a hill. This also included many people, including nurses, who had stayed back to look after the wounded. They had been butchered and brutalised. Eric Fryer, late of the Police Choir, was one of the first Commandoes to land after the war. There was also a Mission to Seaman base there, and the Padre organised soccer matches and sometimes excursions. He would also write to the parents of each Cadet that he met, to say that he had seen them, and that they were in good health. This was much appreciated at home.

Opposite the island was Kowloon on the mainland. Holts

Otaru

had 2 wharves there in a very prominent position, and a short walk to the shops. Cargo work would be very efficient and good natured. Approved traders would set out there stalls on deck, and there was some terrific stuff. They were incredible people with terrific memories, and could remember what you had been interested in, even after long intervals. Inexpensive hand made suits and shirts were a speciality. Measurements on day one. First fitting on day two. Final next day. On one voyage we were invited to visit the tailor's home on our way out in the evening. This was up 3 flights. The whole family was sitting on the floor doing different jobs. Very friendly, a couple of beers, and the suits were ready next day. Lovely people. Camphorwood chests and coffee tables were also very popular, and this was where I bought a coffee table for Dad and Joyce, by request. This is where you bought your Hong Kong basket. A large rectangular cane basket, which you would then cover with canvas, and paint it. Mine is still in the attic. They were much lighter and easier to manage than traditional trunks. Hong Kong was a very busy harbour, with many ships and junks. These are squat looking craft which carried cargo, and on which the whole family would live. Kowloon was close to the border with communist China, and there was a busy trade. This suited everybody. Hong Kong was also a major RN base. The night life was exotic. On one occasion we were in a restaurant bar when some American Marines came in. This was their local leave from the Korean War. Late on they took over the band, and we enjoyed the most tremendous drumming I have ever heard. An experience to remember.

Most of our ships on the Far East run would have done the same voyage, but now the routes would diverge. Some would go to Bangkok. Some north to communist China. Some to the Philippines or Borneo. Some south to Indonesia. Occasionally a ship would go to Pusan in South Korea with war stores. The most popular though, was Japan, which is where we were going.

This involved 5-6 days at sea, and through the Formosan

Strait. China and Formosa were technically at war. This involved a lot of posturing, including war planes and ships, and there were some incidents. It was very grey and windy. It was mid-January, winter, and getting colder. After a few days, the Old Man had us covering the bridge forward windows with paraffin, to stop the spray freezing. It was effective for a while, and so up to the north islands and to Otaru.

Very very cold, and we were at anchor. Cargo into barges, but at 1200 this would stop for 2 hours, Shift change, but also meant that the whole town could take to skiing down the hills. It was an incredible sight, and no, we did not join in. We left after 4 days to go to Yokohama. We were beginning to head home.

TURNING FOR HOME

A run of 2 days, and it started to warm up a bit, but still very cold. Yokohama is the port to Tokyo, and you go alongside. It was within walking distance to the main streets. It was a main recreation area for the American troops from Korea. It was very bright, very gaudy, very noisy, and very busy. Shore leave was great fun, but of course we only had limited funds. The sailors and stewards took full advantage of what was on offer, but most Middies, and nearly all the officers would respect their loved ones at home. We did not want to take home unwelcome legacies. We found the civilians to be very friendly and welcoming, but on the ship they tended to be a bit diffident, almost as if they did not agree that the war should have ended. This is where I purchased the china set, and a small transistor radio. Nothing like this at home. Cameras, binoculars and radio controlled cars were also available. My feelings were a bit mixed when dealing with these people. It was the Japs that had killed my Uncle Eric in a horrific manner in Burma, and a Jap sub that had sunk the ship with my Aunt and Godmother Rosemary on, in the Indian

Ocean. She had married a well known Aussie fighter pilot, Tim Goldsmith, and was on her way to join him in Darwin.

About this time we would start to get details of our destinations and cargoes. This was the Mate's responsibility, and he would have to balance the different types of cargo, weights, where and when loaded, destination order, and the stability of the ship at all times. This could take quite a bit of juggling. There were 3 discharging routes. West coast, usually Liverpool, but sometimes you would go to Glasgow, or Belfast or Dublin. East coast to London, but sometimes you also went to Hull or Edinburgh. Continental, this took you to Antwerp, the port for Brussels, then to Rotterdam, Amsterdam and then to Hamburg.

We now started loading for Liverpool. This was a very popular time for us all. Shimizu was our next stop. A small but beautiful place, surrounded by fields and hedges, with Mount Fujiama as a back drop. Unfortunately the photos don't do it justice. Discharging was now nearly finished, and preparations for loading continued. This entailed shore gangs sweeping the hatches, and we would check that the hatch bilges were clear, and test that they pumped out properly. This sometimes entailed putting your arm up to your shoulder into the bilge, so that you could clear any debris from the pipe end. Not very nice, as you knew, and could see, what was in it. There are no toilets in a cargo hatch. Any damage to cargo equipment would also be repaired if possible.

A short visit to Nagoya, which I thought was a rather grey and bleak industrial area, and then on to Kobe. This was another popular place. More open, with hills in the background, and the people very friendly and more relaxed. Sadly it was devastated by an earthquake a few years ago. On another ship, the *Ajax* later on, we had been there at Christmas. The Mission to Seaman Padre had arranged a midnight communion, which was followed by a visit to his home, a few cans of beer whilst sitting on the floor, a few carols and back on board about 0300. He was an old Conway who had changed his calling, and I had known him there. A very pleasant time.

Back to Hong Kong. Here you would moor to a buoy, or anchor in the roads. Cargo was worked 24/24 and would be loaded from barges or junks, on both sides of the ship. There would be a variety of goods in boxes or bales, but in small quantities, so it was a very busy bustling time.

The ships had 4 or 6 deep tanks. These were special areas which were designed and strengthened in the lower holds for the carriage of liquids, usually latex or palm oil. They would be prepared here. This involved gangs of coollies, who would bring on board long bamboo poles to be constructed into staging. They would scrape and chip in the most inaccessible areas of the tank. Very noisy, very dusty, and very dirty, but they always seemed so cheerful. It would take a couple of days for each tank. The surfaces would then be coated with wax for latex, or rubbed over with hot liquid palm oil as necessary, ready for loading in Malaya. The tanks had large metal lids, which would be closed and bolted to make them watertight. Middies would usually assist the carpenters with this. This was quite a heavy job. If palm oil was involved, then the Engineers would install and test steam pipes. After 4 or 5 days, off to Singapore, where most ships would continue loading.

Middies would assist the deck Mate with supervising the loading. They would be on watches, or a rota. This could involve watching or tallying special cargo, marking blocks of timber with coloured water paint as a colour coding for discharge, helping measure spaces. They would also help, or do the 'tomming off' of free standing blocks of cargo which might collapse at sea. This involved hammering lengths of 4x4 vertical, and building wooden cages or netting, to secure this.

OTHER ROUTES

The other routes outward could have been to Bangkok. This took us through the Gulf of Siam. There was a very large area that you went through, where the surface was covered with thousands of very bright green and red sea snakes about a foot long. They were very venomous, and we didn't stop to see. The port area was over 20 miles from the city, and very remote. On the *Demodocus* we were the first company ship to use the new docks. These were a few hours steaming up a wide and featureless river. We did manage a quick visit to the city, but it was very scruffy, congested and dirty. We didn't have time to visit any of the temples. However, we did discover 'Bangkok Whisky'. Very cheap, and a must try for any connoisseur. It was vile, but you could get used to it, and it was excellent for cleaning tarnished brass. This was important to Middies.

Mainland China was still visited. This could be to Taku Bar. Here you anchored well offshore, and out of sight of the land. Huge barges would come out with the Red Guards and labour. The whole ship would be closed down including the radio room and bar. Personal radios, binoculars etc had to be put into store. We were out of communication. All the labour was dressed in a bluey/grey coloured denim jacket, jeans and caps. Socialism at its purest. They all wore short black rubber boots, where the big toe was separated from the others, like a thumb in a mitten. It was cold, grey and very depressing. Not a place to linger. On one voyage, we did actually go alongside to discharge some heavy cases. These were solemnly lifted on to loose railway lines, and hundreds of dockers would grab ropes and physically haul the boxes along the quay and out of sight. At noon a buzzer would sound. All work stopped immediately, cargo swinging in the breeze, very loud music would start, and everybody solemnly did their Hai Che exercises, or whatever it was called. This will soon be compulsory in this country. Part of healthy living and

Demodocus

good socialism. After a while the buzzer would sound again, and they resumed their activities. Nothing was said or instructions given. The guards did of course observe. We were exempt as being past redemption.

Shanghai. This had once been a major, and very busy, international commercial city, with a strong British presence. It was now neglected, and looked very drab and grey. However, many of the buildings had once been very impressive. It is a few hundred miles up the Yangtse River, through a very wide estuary surrounded by featureless mud flats. Once again everything was locked up, and there were guards on board. We were on the *Flintshire*, and we went alongside to work cargo. The dock was walking distance to the city centre, but there wasn't much to do there. All alcohol was banned. However, the authorities did allow one bar to serve visiting seamen. Recognition at last. Some of us decided to sample the hospitality, and I went ashore with the Chief Steward early, and the rest came later. The bar was very basic, but friendly, and we supped the beer steadily. The others joined us, but it soon ran out. We didn't know that it was rationed. We then had the option of Vodka, or more Vodka. It was good stuff, and possibly came from the cellars of the closed Embassies. We did not normally drink this, but with orange squash and ice, it was very pleasant. The music was old western, mainly Elvis. The bar closed just after 2200. We were OK until we got to the door. Fresh air, a smoky atmosphere, a strange drink is a volatile mix. It affected us all. We headed back to base, and I can remember pointing out a narrow passage that we had to go down. After that nothing. Next morning, I was told that the guard at the bottom of the gangway demanded to see our ID cards. I was not able to produce this, and he actually had the catch off his sub machine gun. Thankfully one of my colleagues realised what was happening, had seen it in my top pocket, grabbed it, and thrust it under his nose. Reluctantly he let us on board. Apparently there were bonus points to be had

At the peak, November 1955

for shooting incapable British cadets. Next morning I found myself on the settee. I hadn't been sick, and actually felt quite well. However, there was a cyclone warning, and the ship was moved to buoys in the middle of the river. We were all a bit fragile. We put out all the wires and ropes that we could. Traffic movements gradually stopped. The wind started to pick up, and after dinner we went on to sea watches. The engines were put on stand by, and crew stationed at each end with a Mate and Middie, with fire axes. The gangway was lifted clear. It was now a matter of waiting. We were able to rotate attendance, so that people were fresh but available.

The *Flintshire* was a Sam boat, or Liberty ship. These vessels were mass produced in America to replace lost tonnage. They were very basic, almost glorified barges. If they completed one voyage across the Atlantic, they had justified themselves. Just shows how bad things were. There were so many, that they were named after the wives of the shipbuilders. After the war, some were acquired by the company, refurbished, renamed, and strengthened. Some were in service 30 years later. They had a reputation for breaking in half just forward of the bridge under certain weather conditions. They had steam engines, almost like a sowing machine, and were very quiet. Cruising speed of about 12 knots; that is, with a following wind, and going downhill. When we had left Birkenhead, I was on the bridge. When we rang full ahead, I was expecting the usual surge. I looked over the side, and the water hadn't moved. It was going to be a long slow voyage. What we could have done had there been a major problem, in a confined area, with many obstacles, a rampaging river, and very high winds, is very questionable. But, we had every confidence in the ship, the arrangements, and each other. We were away 4 ½ months.

After a day or so the weather abated, and when the river had settled down, we set off to sea. When the pilot has been dropped there is a sense of relief, and we could open everything up and get back to normal. Civilisation rejoined.

Flintshire at sea

Tropical uniform

Flintshire foredeck

*Hitching a ride
in the Red Sea*

The Yangtse of course is where the *Amethyst* had been in trouble previously. A few years later, a 2nd Mate was arrested and accused of spying. Apparently he had made some notes on the one river chart that we were allowed to use. As navigating officer he had corrected the position of some of the buoys which had been moved. That was part of his job. He was very conscientious. He was a contemporary of mine. He was paraded through the city in the back of an open lorry through a hostile mob. There was jeering, spitting, jostling, and he feared for his life. He then spent 2 years in prison. Hardly a rest home. Where was HM Diplomatic core? What was done to help him, or was it simply dismissed as a small diplomatic incident. Years later, when I joined Ocean Fleets, I met him in Tilbury. He was a shadow of a man. Thin, pale, and no personality, no humour. The company were very loyal to him, and kept him employed. He was married with a couple of kids.

On another ship we went to Tsingtao. This was on the coast, and had been an up-market holiday resort. It had seen better days, but the people were much more relaxed and friendly. It was in a pleasant Bay with space for 2 ships alongside. There were also some gunboats at anchor. The shops were pretty drab and mainly second-hand antiques. There was also a club that we could visit. This was run by a lovely man and his family. During the First World War he had been part of the gangs that had collected the dead and body bits in battle zones. He bore no resentment, and loved the Brits. He made us very welcome. The ship ahead was British, the *City of Ottawa*. Their voyages were much longer than ours, up to 2 years away, so they were glad to see some friendly faces. We met up in the evening. After much conviviality it was decided that there should be a Test match. The floor was smooth marble and tables were moved to one side. The ball was a ping pong ball, and the bat a vodka bottle. Empty of course. This was serious stuff. A lively ball, hard surface, dodgy umpiring, and an atmosphere that made the Aussies look like a bunch of pussy cats. It was going well, we were chasing,

I was getting the hang of the wicket and hit a glorious straight drive which sped to the far wall. Unfortunately so did the bat. It slipped out of my hands, and smashed into the wall behind it. Stunned silence. The debris was immediately swept up, and an emergency conference held. Out of respect and regard to our hosts, who had been thoroughly enjoying the proceedings, it was decided the match be declared an honourable draw, due to equipment malfunction. We then adjourned to the bar and finished off the evening. They sailed next day, and we a few days later.

A few months before joining the *Flintshire*, Dad had given me the dates of his next leave to the UK. We hadn't met for 4 years, so I raised this with the office. They said they would see what they could do. When I was appointed to the ship, I realised that the dates of return did not coincide, so I mentioned this to them. Don't worry they said. After leaving China, we received a message to say that I would leave the ship in Makasar, a small port in the Celebes. On arrival I was told that a bus would collect me next day for my flight, and to have all my gear with me. I was also told that it would have to go through an area of terrorist activity, and that the driver had instructions to drive very quickly if anything happened. Well the road was rutted with deep potholes, and at full pace, a bike would have overtaken us. I do confess that I clutched my sextant box very tightly, and hoped it would provide some sort of protection. Thankfully we arrived safely in a large field in a big clearing, and at the far end there was a corrugated tin hut. This was the check in and departure lounge. A small plane was parked nearby, so we stopped next to it, and boarded. The engines started up, and we took off. My first flight. It was run by a Dutch firm, Garuda Airlines. About 30 seats, very clean, tidy and bright. The crew were friendly and efficient, and soon a cup of coffee was helping the proceedings. What a view. We weren't flying very high, and could see the islands, beaches, reefs, everything. It was breathtaking. We were going to Surabaya on Java to refuel, about 2 hours away, and then onwards to Djakarta. On touch down I was met by a clerk from the office and he told me that we were running late, and that I would have to stay overnight. He took me to a small, but clean and basic hotel. It didn't do evening meals, but it was arranged that he would collect me later, and take me into the bazaar. This created mixed feelings, as the Indonesians had a reputation for being a bit knifey, very volatile, and did not like whites after their independence from the Dutch. He reassured me, tapped his knife, and we had a very pleasant evening. I did notice that he did have a few words with different people as we went round. Next morning I was put on a different plane, and it was only a short journey to the main airport. Here I was met and taken to the airline hotel, to await for the flight in the evening. I was also told that a party had been arranged for me by the office the night before, which carried on anyway. Ah well, another opportunity to foster international relations bites the dust. I was 17 and unattached. Later I was ferried to the International airport. Bigger than the other one, but small compared to modern ones. The flight was behind schedule, but as twilight closed in, there was a silver flash in the distance as the sun caught the tail fins, and the QUANTAS Super Constellation landed. This had 4 props, and 3 distinctive tail fins. A beautiful sight, and no sound. We were bundled on board, there weren't many spare seats, and I sensed a resentment to the new passengers. The residents had been on board for a long time, and they were very tired. On take off the lights were dimmed, it was dark outside, and we just sat there for 2 hours or so. It was a bit airless. At Singapore I was taken to Connell House, as my next ship, the *Ulysses*, had sailed 5 hours earlier. Next day I was flown up to Kuala Lumpur.

She was one of 2 ships purchased by the company when Silver Line closed down. A different design to our usual Blueys. More comfortable, and she had air conditioning. A very desirable posting. Blue Flue was not enthusiastic about this

Ulysses

Bohihan

Logs at Bohihan

mollycoddling. The atmosphere was relaxed, and I was made
to feel at home, and settled in quickly. They obviously knew of
my background.

When we went to the office, I was naturally full of gratitude,
and I was given the number of days leave that I could expect.
Contact was made with Dad, who had taken over a cottage in
the New Forrest near Lyndhurst. We had a very special week
together, with Joyce, Hester and Richard. In a sense we were
strangers, and from very different backgrounds, but families do
gel. The next time we met was a few years later at Seberham
in Cumberland, after they had left Kenya. This was when they
found and bought Greenrow. I was there.

The Rajang River in Sarawak was a place that we weren't
too keen on. You went quite a long way up the river to a long
sweeping bend, with foliage to the water all the way up. No
human settlements in sight. Here there was space for 3 or 4
ships to anchor. Rafts of logs were floated down and you lifted
them straight from the water. It was very very hot and sultry,
uncomfortably so. Cargo was 24/24. At twilight, a Middie would
take 2 lit hurricane lamps by boat, and place them in front of two
trees that had had some white paint splashed on. This involved
clambering 20 or 30 yards up very muddy and slippery river
banks. There were all sorts of eyes and slithererings around
you. Not a place to linger. These marks were so that the duty
mate could check whether the ship was dragging anchor during
the night. The ship's deck lights attracted all the flying insects,
and some were very large. Four engined jobs. It was not very
pleasant. Having said that, in the early hours, two hours before
dawn, everything would go silent and still, and it was very cool
and pleasant. Even cargo work would peter out as the rafts were
finished. It was a magical time. However, all good things come
to an end, and soon the new day would start. Agents, boats, and
new shifts, including the day insects. Bedlam and noisy.

Ships would also go to the north of Borneo. This was more

environmently pleasant and interesting, with nice beaches and coconut trees to the waters edge. The hinterland led onto dramatic mountain ranges. There were bays with numerous islands, some small, and some large. We visited Labuan and Sandakan. Here you anchored off the beach, and loaded logs from the sea. It was more relaxed and less intense than the other ports, and work finished at twilight. There were boats to take you ashore, and it was good to be able to have a swim, wander about, and we had a soccer game against a local Chinese team. They were pretty useful, but it was good fun. There was a sense of peace and tranquillity. An idyllic spot. Years later, I heard that these had been the sites of POW massacres when the Japs left. This has been felt by other people elsewhere when visiting horrific battlefields. Does this mean that there are forces of nature that we can't recognise, or understand?

Bohihan was an island in a large bay surrounded by many others. There was an Agent's office and an area where logs were gathered and made up into rafts. Many of the crew wanted to have swim, but we were warned that the bay was full of shoals of barracuda, and that they attacked on sight. A shark will tend to swim around an eye up its next meal. Some of us were invited to the office, for a run down of what happened there, and ended up wandering around the floating logs. We were warned to watch out for snakes. Thankfully there were no incidents.

Manila in the Philippines was approached up a river, which was quite wide in places. You went close to and past the island of Corregidor. This is where General McArthur and his forces were surrounded and holed up by the Japs for some considerable time, and not taken. The island is totally exposed, and it was said that if a rat moved it was shot up. How they endured and survived is unbelievable. The word courage just does not describe it. It was declared a memorial.

Some ports were noted for serious pilfering problems, and there had been some bad experiences. On one occasion there was a briefing, and we were solemnly sent down a hatch each. All hands on deck with a Mate, Purser and Radio Officer all in attendance. In my hatch there were cartons of tinned peaches. Very desirable loot. After a while you start chatting to the labour. My Filipino is impeccable. Out of the corner of my eye there was a small disturbance. I would suddenly notice, and there were hoots of laughter when I admonished them. This became a game of tick, and we had great fun. The deck patrol would regularly shout down, everything OK, yes I would reply. As the day progressed, I became aware that there were problems in the other hatches, and 2 of the Middies had had to be brought out. When we closed up, 3 cartons were damaged in my hatch, and about 6 cans had disappeared. The Purser who was in charge of checking was very impressed. When we were debriefed, after what had been a very difficult day for everybody, I was ticked off for not summoning help. Secretly I think there was relief that the problems had not been worse.

HOMEWARDS

All ships on the Far East run would load and fill up in Malaya. Sawn timber. Bales of rubber, hemp, fibre, cotton waste. Bags of rice, copra, sago, desiccated coconut and pepper. Bundles of hides and canes. Scrap metal. Empty welding gas cylinders. Anything.

The bales were strips of rubber compressed, and then covered in white powder. They were awkward shapes, so, difficult to walk over. If they got wet, they became very slippery.

Bagged cargo usually had to have channels built into the stow, for ventilation. Sometimes small wooden frames would be used to stop collapsing.

Copra was the flesh of coconuts which had been dried in the sun. It had a pungent smell, and it attracted little black beetles.

These got all over the ship, and gave nasty little nips. Bit of a nuisance.

The hides were in awkward shaped bundles, and if they got wet, were not very pleasant.

The deep tanks would be filled. Latex was quite easy, just fill up and close down. It gave a very strong smell of ammonia. You always left a space at the top of a tank of liquid to allow for expansion. This is known as an 'ullage space.'

Palm or coconut oil needed heating and looking after. Hence the steam pipes. The temperature had to be checked 3 times a day. This involved a long brass chain which had 2 or 3 thermometers attached at different heights. These would be passed down a sounding pipe from the top deck. They had to be hauled up very quickly, to stop the lower readings being affected by the upper ones. It was a messy job, as you were on the open deck, it was always windy, and you always got splashed with the hot sticky liquid.

Ships were usually full after Penang, but if you had some space, then sometimes you would call at Colombo, in Ceylon, for chests of tea. On one occasion when we had piles of logs on deck, a 3 foot snake was discovered near the pilot ladder. A group of experts soon assembled, but 2 sailors hit it with a metal bar and bundled it into a sack. They were about to throw it over the side, when the Doctor, who had been retired, asked if he could have it for research. He put it into his surgery. He of course went ashore with some friends. During the morning there was a small injury to a docker. He was taken by the 3rd mate to the surgery. There they were greeted by a very undead, unhappy reptile, coiled around the soil pipe of the basin. Spitting and hissing viciously. Time for a quick exit. Casualty sent ashore. On his return, the Doctor was given a very severe reprimand for endangering the crew. What we couldn't understand, was that we had been at sea for a few days, without any inkling that it was there, and in an area where we had walked and worked daily. Thankfully this was an isolated incident.

Shortly after leaving Penang, just north of Sumatra, we went through an area which we knew as the 'Captain's graveyard'. This is not far from where the recent big Tsunami had started. Apparently, over the years a number of Masters had disappeared there. They led a very lonely life, with huge responsibilities and pressure. It was a time when we were all washed out, but glad to be on our way home. Very sad really.

Soon day work restarted. Everywhere was cleaned, scrubbed, and painted. This included the masts, all derrick posts, and the funnel. Middies would usually attend to the boat deck, including the lifeboats and all lifebelts. The names would have to be redone by free hand, and we found the Chinese Pencils to be very useful.

Lifeboat and fire drill would be held weekly at sea. The signal would be given on the whistle and alarm bells. This was 7 or more short blasts, followed by a long one. Everybody would go to their boat stations, wearing their life jackets, be checked off, and then one of the boats would be swung out. By law, cargo ships had to have sufficient boats on each side, for everybody on board. With passenger ships, it was in total, but supplemented by life rafts. Fire drill would follow, and a site selected in different places each time. Fire hoses would be rigged and tested. The nearest extinguishers brought out and sometimes set off. Some thought these exercises were a bit tame and pointless, but they did mean that equipment was checked, and used on a regular basis. They also took place in off duty time. All crew members had attended fire courses. Damage and clogging up was a real possibility. The engine room water tight door would also be closed, and then opened, from the bridge.

Once a voyage, the ship would be stopped in mid-ocean, and the motor lifeboat lowered. This was to test the emergency radio. The ship would then disappear over the horizon. Once completed, you were then picked up. It was a bit eeery, even in a flat calm. Sometimes I would be on the bridge, and nearly always you could see a big shark not far away. This happened often if the ship stopped.

Animals were often carried, which the Middies would look after. There would be a small payment at the end. Always useful. Usually pet dogs, but on one occasion it was a wild cat, lynx, and Bengal tiger. These were in small cages on the top of the poop. The tiger was fine, but the other 2 were vicious. We didn't look after these. However, a .303 rifle was put on board, just in case, together with 3 very greased up bullets. Nobody checked to see if anybody could use it. The 4th Mate was in the RNR, so he was delegated to be the marksman, but thankfully not needed. On the Aggy, there was a steady trade in race horses to Singapore. I shared responsibility in looking after 'Lindos'. She occasionally won.

The Chinese greasers lived in the poop accommodation. They would put opened eggs on to large food trays, on the top, outside in the open. There they would fry and stay until we docked. A sought out delicacy in Chinatown. Much enhanced by spray, soot from the funnel, and splashes from washing and painting activities. You don't see that bit on the 'tele', do you?

Passing Gibraltar homewards was always significant. You were only 3 or 4 days from home! The RN signal station would call you up by Morse lamp. 'What ship, where bound'? This information would be passed to India Building. Home soon!

The weather would still be fine, but as you turned north it would get chillier, and back into 'blues'. The coast of Spain gave way to the Biscay. There was usually a bit of a weather welcome. On one trip I remember talking to the Chief Steward, when one of his juniors asked him, 'when will we dock? He looked out of his porthole and asked me, is that Finisterre? Yes I said, 'what are the tide times'? About 11ish, he thought for a moment and said, the night tide on Tuesday. We did. On the bridge the Old Man and 2nd Mate were poring over tide tables, current charts and weather forecasts so that they could send the ETA to HO. Do we sometimes get too bogged down with detail? When standing back and taking a broader picture is just as useful.

We picked up the Pilot at Holyhead; some very welcome mail, past the Great Orme, and into the Mersey, what a beautiful sight. Tie up in Gladstone Dock. FWE. Customs visits, tidy and clean up, instructions, heavy gear to the lorry for transport to Lime Street station. Pandemonium, and then orft to HO for interviews, travel voucher and expenses. Birkenhead to Bootle in just over 3 months.

OTHER SPECIAL SHIPS

M.V. Agamemnon (aka Aggy)

All Mates and Middies were expected to do a long voyage. Probably 6 to 12 months away. This meant going out to join a ship that was permanently stationed abroad. You would take a main line ship out to a suitable port, and just simply switch over. He, or they, would take your place and go home.

For my second voyage, at the office interview, I was introduced to new companions, and told that we would join the *Ashcan* outwards, but be transferred to the *Agamemnon* when convenient. She had been on the Far East to USA run, but was going to be refitted, in Hong Kong, to do the Malaya round Aussie run. We got on very well, and were looking forward to this trip. The two ships' dates did not match up, and we were back to Singapore, before we were told to join the M.V. *Adrastus* outwards to go up to Hong Kong.

She already had 4 Miiddies onboard, so we were allocated some empty passenger cabins. We were expected to do some work, but we were only there for 4 days, so it was light. It was here that I first met David Waring. The Master was very enlightened, and allowed the Middies to have some cider.

Aggy

Nick, Cardiff and John

Many would not. It was David's 17th birthday; nobody was on watches, so we had a very enjoyable evening, particularly David. This was aided by some bottles of beer from the Mates, who would normally send some over for special events. On arrival in Hong Kong we were quickly transferred to the Aggy. She was in Taikoo drydock, at the far end of the harbour. Not very pleasant, there was no power, and we had to use the toilet and shower facilities on the dock side. These were very basic. We were there for 10 days, and gradually the facilities were returned to us. We did some light jobs, and had access to a 2 man wooden outrigger canoe. This was great fun. What sharks? We didn't see any. Eventually we sailed to Singapore, and started to load there, and then around Malaya.

The Aggy was built in 1929, was twin screw, and had a very full history. Originally built for Blue Flue, she was taken over to be a minelayer during the war, and worked north of Scotland. When this finished, she was converted to be an Amenity ship in the Far East, to give the Military some respite. This included a theatre and a brewery. However the war ended just as she was going out to start her new career. She was then converted back for general trading, and returned to the company. She was always a happy ship. Being old, you possibly didn't expect too much. All departments worked well together, and the ship ran smoothly. A Chinese crew, this always helped. The ships would be immaculate, food superb, and they did your laundry, for a reasonable cost. The Old Man was Gentleman Johnston, a lovely man, who had commanded destroyers during the war. Aussie next, is there a heaven at sea?

The halfdeck was on the main deck next to a main alley way, and No. 3 hatch. It was always noisy and busy in port, but we made ourselves comfortable.

My first port in Australia was Fremantle. Low lying, sandy, very hot, always windy, but gave the impression of being clean and in a desert area. This is the main port for the state capital,

Perth. There were some lovely beaches nearby, which we tried to visit if we could. You had to be careful because of the dangerous surf. The ship had a smaller motor lifeboat, and on one occasion we were sent off for the afternoon, to a sand bank to collect sand in half barrels, for cleaning the decks. This was a very pleasant break. On another, on a Sunday, we went up the river towards the city, found a nice beach and had a swim. The local families were all down, and it was almost like being at home. Perhaps a little warmer and settled. The MCC tour started there. The local radios were full of it; they expected to dish out another hammering. It was the Tyson tour. On his first over they were horrified, 'Jeeez, where did that ball go? It was a while before they could pick the ball up. We loved it of course, and yes, he did well. We sent a request for a record to be played, and they could not get the hang of the ship's name. We thoroughly enjoyed their discomfort. Our route followed the tour. In Melbourne I was able to see them for a day's play v An Aussie XI. Lindwall, Miller, Johnston, Toshack, Morris, Hassett. Hutton, Washbrook, Edrich, Compton, May, Cowdrey, Graveney, Evans, Bedser, and Tyson. Legends all, in a glorious setting. A 17 year old was very happy. The ground was huge, and geared up for large crowds. To get a beer involved putting a deposit on a plastic glass, going to another counter, and paying for a squirt of the amber nectar from a tap on a hose. Very quick, but it was a bit splashy.

Next we went to Port Adelaide. This is almost 30 miles from the city. A bit too far to travel to. However, the Mission to Seaman Padre always visited, and usually invited us to join his family for Sunday lunch. Much appreciated. All the Aussie ports had a Mission clubhouse. They tried to organise dances and other social activities, as well as regular church services. All dances would have a short period of worship. They were well attended by all hands. There were some pairings off, some subsequent marriages, and even immigration. A bit like Liverpool.

Melbourne is at the top of a large bay. You have to go through quite a narrow entrance, and the change in weather and temperature could be very dramatic. Melbourne can get very chilly, particularly if you are not expecting it, and are in the wrong clothes. There are 2 ports, but not too far from the city. The buildings are large, and almost Victorian. It was a nice place to visit, but the pubs shut at 1800. Much socialising and barbecuing at home.

Sydney, what an approach you have, through the bay, and then under the bridge. There was a figure suspended underneath it in the middle, where we had to pass. Thankfully it was a student prank. Here I met up with the Goldsmith's, parents of Tim, arranged by Granny. They were very welcoming and glad to meet me. Someone from the 'ole country'. A much prized contact. Mr G was a typical hard working Aussie, but Mrs G was more English in attitude and loyalty. Many of the women tried to create 'Little England ' homes. These were very comfortable and homely, and admired. The food, and particularly the meat, was superb. They lived in a bungalow in the northern suburbs. This involved a train journey over the bridge. This was fascinating. What did catch my eye though, was the notices at each end of the carriages, with pictures of different snake bites, and instructions what to do. The local radio would sometimes announce that, a 'brown' had been seen. You don't hear that from Eric Smith.

On one voyage they laid on a meeting for me with Tim in a nearby bar. It was very strained. He was a very famous war hero; he had been shot down and wounded badly a few times, had lost his wife in tragic circumstances, had remarried and then was trying to live a new life. Here was a 17 year old, a total stranger, who couldn't remember his Aunt and Godmother, and both of us trying to make small talk. After a while we did thaw out, but I don't know if the meeting did him any good. To me it was a privilege. He died at 48, and the streets of Sydney were

Nick and I in outrigger

The 4 Middies

*Lindos arrives,
Singapore*

closed for the funeral procession. His brother Christopher and wife Jenny, were totally different, and made me very welcome. He was a Commander in the Royal Australian Navy, and on the carrier *Melbourne*. They were in port, and they took me over for an informal Mess Dinner. Great fun.

Brisbane was our last port. It is a few miles up a river, low lying, and very green. Always a happy place.

The Middies took over the hatch cleaning and tomming off, or cargo securing. After a while we got on top of this, and it became quite easy, and a bit of a challenge. If things were quiet whilst cargo watching, we would get on with odd jobs. Made life a lot easier.

For the second voyage we went north and east of Australia, and down past the Barrier Reef. You couldn't see much, but you knew from the charts how dangerous it could be. We went to Cairns and Townsville, both small towns with a few shops, couple of bars, police station and a rail track down the middle of the High Street. They are a bit different now. We did go to an outdoor cinema, a Western I think. What an experience.

The voyage continued clockwise round Australia and back to Malaya. On one voyage we passed close to the island of Krakatoa, the scene of one of the world's biggest bangs, only a couple of hundred years ago. It felt a bit sinister, and recent pictures on TV suggest that it is now a lot bigger. Is another one brewing? On this passage I started to get some abdominal discomfort. The Master and Chief Steward became a bit concerned that it might be appendicitis. This is a major worry for seafarers. In Singapore I saw a doctor, who thought it might be a grumbling appendix, but that I was OK for now, and that he would arrange for a specialist appointment on our return. Light duties only.

The discharging and loading were routine, but we were to spend Xmas Day at anchor in Port Swettenham. The only 2 days in the year that it closed down. We were on our own, gangway

Taikoo drydock,
July '54

Sydney Harbour Bridge

Townsville,
September '54

up, and the only watch keeping was in the engine room, and done by the Junior Engineers, in turn. We had a very quiet day. Late in the afternoon No. 3 hatch was set out for a buffet. We all assembled in our best shore going tropical gear, some music was found for a gramophone, and copious quantities of the amber nectar appeared. The buffet was traditional festive fare, done beautifully, but also crayfish, small lobsters actually, baked in a light cheese sauce. Did we enjoy that! It was a lovely tropical evening, and it did cool down a bit. One of the benefits of these voyages, was that the food was collected locally. Sadly I had to take things a bit easy, but I did enjoy the occasion.

In Singapore the specialist decided that I would have to have an operation, but in the New Year. The port closed down and most people went ashore. Because I had to be careful, it was decided that I would stay on board to help keep ship. There was some sensible drinking, after all we were on duty, but at 2350, it was all hands to the bridge. It was a beautiful, balmy, still, tropical evening. At midnight, all hell let lose. 40 ships simultaneously sounding their whistles, hooters, all of them, what a sound, what an experience. Next day the engineers complained that all the compressed air bottles were empty.

The Agent took me to the Military Hospital; I should have had a private room, but ended up on a general ward. In the next bed was a young Japanese cadet. We became quite friendly and compared experiences, including our understanding of the war. The new young had different attitudes to their elders. The op was a success, in fact one of the first keyhole incisions, and commented on by surgeons later. Recuperation took 10 days in Connell House. A nice room and it was a quiet time.

The trip home was on the *Antilochus*. It was uneventful, and I was on light duties. In all, I was away for 9½ months. Thoroughly enjoyable, but not for the marrieds!

S.S Troilus

Another Sam boat, but with a difference. It was the time of the first Suez crisis. Ships were having to sail round the Cape of Good Hope. Voyages were much longer. Problems were arising with reliefs and leave periods. It was promotion for me to 4th Mate. A big increase in salary. Back to the Far East. She had been launched as *'Martha C Thomas'*, sailed as *'Samharle'*, hence Samboats, then became the *'Troilus'*.

It took us 11 days to reach Dakar, in Senegal, to refuel. Then 21 days round to Durban. I was on the 4-8 watch with the Chief Officer, and we got on very well. Before sailing, I had written to Dad telling him that we were going to Durban, and was there anybody there that I should know about. Vaguely, as a child, I was aware of some family in South Africa. We docked at 0500, it was a lovely morning, and I was rather surprised to see some white men handling the ropes, and an African in charge of the tug. This isn't what we were told in the papers. What about apartheid? As we were only refuelling it was quiet for us, and after I had been given a large bundle of mail, I retired to my cabin and opened the first letter. Almost immediately there was a knock on my door. Two gentlemen stood there, and said, 'We are your uncles'. This was a bit of a shock at 0630. I made a hurried excuse, and dashed back into the room. A quick flip through the letters, and there were 2 from Dad. Panic opening, and there it was, I have 2 brothers there, Herbert and Robin. I composed myself and greeted them happily. They asked if they could take me ashore for the day? A quick word with the c/o, who spoke to the Old Man, and permission was granted. After a shower and breakfast, they picked me up and we drove around the city. This included a visit to their office. They ran a security firm that looked after hospitals, shops, offices docks, and government departments. The guards were taken from the Zulus, and were their main source of employment. After the Zulu war, they had been shunned. Durban tended to be British by connection and sympathy, and the family were anti-apartheid. In fact, Herbert's wife Eleanor was often threatened with prison. They lived a long way out, so there wasn't time to see her. After a coffee we drove round the outskirts and in time to watch some of Natal playing Transvaal in a state match. I was very impressed with Goddard, a young left arm bowler, who later did very well. Then we went to Robin's house and met Flo. She was a large but lovely woman and character. Also their 2 daughters, Elizabeth and Jennifer. A big welcome, and we spent some time there. Then it was time to get back. We sailed at 1700, due east out into the Indian Ocean. It was twilight, my watch, and it was sad to see the lights of the city receding astern of us. What a day. Time to read the rest of the mail.

Penang 21 days later. The voyage could now start. It was a normal discharge, but when we started loading, we went to Tjillitjap on the south coast of Java. It is approached up a short river with steep cliffs to either side, but these do level down to a single wharf. We were to load 3,500 tons of manganese iron ore. This is like a heavy black grit. There were a couple of small mounds at the end of the dock, but these were supplemented by 2 trains of wagons. It was all done by hand. Gangs of men and women would take a small flat basket on their heads to have a couple of scoops put in, and then scurry to tip it into a big wicker basket, which was hoisted and tipped into the hatches. Another gang would level it out in the hatch. To spread the weight we had to use 5 hatches. It took 10 days. It was here that I acquired the 2 cages of Java Sparrows from a vendor. They were so unique, with a very distinctive song, and much fun, but they did need looking after. Probably wouldn't do it these days. It seemed a good idea at the time. Care has to be taken when loading heavy cargo, too much low down can cause a pendulum effect on the ship's stability, which can result in exaggerated rolling and damage. Sensible loading thereafter can offset this.

Java sparrows

Loading iron ore at Tjilitjap

The ship did not have radar, because of inadequate power. When we passed Spain the weather closed over, and we had moderate gales. We were not able to get sights or establish our position for 10 days. We had to turn east to go up the English Channel. This had to be done by dead reckoning, or guestimate. This was an anxious time, as Ushant, a low lying point on the north west of France, that you had to use as a marker, was covered with wrecks that had got it wrong. We had got it right.

We left the ship in Rotterdam at the end of April. We had been away for 6 ½ months. Some leave, and as my sea time was now sufficient, it was time to start on my 2nd Mates certificate in London. I was aged just over 20.

GIRLFRIENDS

Sooner or later, most of us acquired a girlfriend. Relationships were never going to be easy. Most of the courtship would be done by letter, with just a few snatched periods of leave. There were a few breakdowns, and when you are away, these make for a very difficult time. There isn't much you can do, as time in communication could take so long. A break-up could be devastating. However, if you did find somebody who was understanding, supportive, patient, loyal, and lovely, then she was idolised and worshipped. Everybody respected this. It took a special woman to take on a seafarer. Having said that, it did seem that for some inexplicable reason we were considered to be a desirable catch. This was quite understandable, of course.

A few friendships had started during childhood or school days, but many through later socials. Some of course petered out.

Atlantic House in Liverpool was a Seamen's Mission run by the RCs. It had a very good reputation for welcome and facilities, and was considered to be a safe place to go to. Dances were held every evening, and the Priests would keep a very stern eye on proceedings. A colleague and I had a couple of beers and decided to join in. We broke up a circle of girls who were chattering, and asked for a dance. This was very pleasant. We asked the same partners up again, and it turned out that they had come in together. This was very nice. Hello Dot. When we asked if we could escort them home, we were told of the very strict rules about fraternising, but we were also told of where the bus stop round the corner was. We were far from home and very vulnerable. The rest is history. We seemed to get on so well and naturally. The other two didn't last long, and in fact Pat later immigrated to Australia. We, are still going strong.

There may have been some ups and downs, but overall, there has always been the commitment to the marriage, the family, the home, and many, many happy times. Is this how it should be?

Dot

Certificated Deck Officer

November 1957 to February 1959

My return to seafaring was delayed, due to a fractured collar bone.

Results of the 2nd Mates exam were not posted to you; you had to phone to see if they were available, and then visit the nearest MN Dock Office to be told your fate. This involved a train journey from Tunbridge Wells to Charing Cross, a tube to Aldgate, and a long walk. You had to pass all sections, with a minimum mark on each, and a minimum overall average. If you failed any part, you were not told which. Just a curt 'failed'. Thankfully it was a grumpy 'Passed'. I have never been very impressed with civil servants, or office clerks, since. However, I was pretty confident, but you never know. At 20 years and 4 months, I was one of the youngest to do so. There weren't many people around, but a couple of us did meet up and celebrate the culmination of almost 6 years of blood, sweat, and tears, politely referred to as career training. Having said that, it had been a wonderful experience, and Blue Flue were great teachers.

Next day, was a Saturday. Cricket. You have been selected to play in the 2nd XI, away. Meet at the club coach, a very dilapidated vehicle. It had been raining incessantly for some time. Most games in Kent had been called off, but not ours. Was I in a reasonable state to play? But of course you do, can't let the side down, Old Boy. We lost the toss and were invited to field. It was very soggy, and I found myself at fine leg, midway to the boundary. There was a quiet start, but unexpectedly the ball ballooned up off the bat edge, headed very high, and headed vaguely into my part of the field. I lolloped off towards it, when I realised that I might be able to get close, so I lunged. Some said it was like a swallow swooping. The ball was in my right hand, until the shoulder hit the ground, I felt the bone go, and the ball spilt out. Deathly silence. A dropped catch. A visit to the Emergency Department, and a rather shocked journey home. Six weeks recuperation, with funds running short. Blue Funnel were sympathetic, but not very impressed.

Jason

November 1957 to July 1958

Jason was one of four regular Aussie boats. A popular run. Slightly bigger than the other fleet ships, about 10,000 gross tons, mainly refrigerated cargo, steam turbine with a 17.5 knots service speed, and carried 32 passengers. That meant she had to have a doctor on board. There was a very good arrangement whereby physician, desirous of experience in far flung areas could go one way, and the heirs of the convicts could sample civilisation on the return. This worked well, and I made a few friends. One was John Kneebone from Adelaide. The steam engines made for a much more comfortable ride, as there wasn't the vibration and noise of the diesels. Whilst the rules about fraternising with passengers still applied, there seemed to be a more relaxed atmosphere. We joined in Birkenhead, and I was Extra Third Mate. This meant that I was on the 4-8 watch with the Chief Officer. We would share navigation and lookout duties, and as he and I became more confident, he would leave me on my own. This paid off in the Indian Ocean. The weather was gorgeous, and he would come onto the bridge at 0600 for his cup of tea and round of toast, whilst I could have a swim, sea temp. 82 degrees, and then get changed into my normal white uniform. The Old Man was Willie Hole, a huge person, with a reputation for being very hard and strict, and possibly a little traditional. I learnt to like and respect him, and we got on well. Learnt a lot. One of my jobs was to open and check every fire extinguisher once a week. This was usually done once a voyage. Can you be too careful?

At sea the day would start at 0345 with a tap on the side of the bunk, usually the Middy. At 0355 there would be a reminder. It was an unwritten rule that you were never late on watch. Uniform rules were relaxed, and comfortable and clean clothes were allowed. The bridge would be very dark, but a pot of tea and some stale sandwiches would be ready. At night no lights would be allowed to shine forward of the superstructure, as this would inhibit the vision of the lookout and watch keeper. After a period of adjustment, it is amazing what you can see on the darkest of nights. The 2nd Mate would finish off his navigation and log book whilst you adjusted, and then point out the movements of all the ships that were visible. Then give you the course, compass errors, and navigation facilities available, together with any special instructions. There was also a Night Orders book that had to be read and initialled. This was the Master's notes to the Officers, usually written before he retired to bed. He was always on call. You were then on your own. Lookout and ship safety were the first priority. If in sight of land, positions would be taken every half hour by visual bearings of prominent charted objects, such as lighthouses, headlands, hills, jetties etc. These could be very accurate with practice, but this did depend on the compass errors being known. Every watch, and after every alteration of course, the compasses would be checked using the stars, or moon, or sun, and recorded. This would take about ten minutes, but you still had to keep a lookout. All the bridge compasses were compared regularly. The Master would usually ask for a call when approaching an alter course. There would be three sailors on a watch. One on the wheel, one

In my cabin

Adelaide river

forward on lookout, and a spare. He could be summoned by a whistle. He would keep their kettle going. They would rotate their duties, and report to the duty officer when this took place. This stopped any dozing off. Ship safety and all that. Keeping awake in the middle of the night after broken routines, broken sleep, heavy work, a trip ashore, could sometimes be very difficult for anybody.

About 0600, a steward would appear with a cup of tea and a round of toast. Very welcome. If out at sea, star sights would be taken during twilight, as soon as the horizon was firm enough, and you could still pick out the stars. It could take up to half an hour to calculate a position. A lookout still had to be kept, but as light strengthened you could move into the front of the bridge, and the forward sailor would be stood down.

At 0800 the 3rd Mate would appear, and the handover procedure repeated. Time for a shave, shower, and breakfast. Usually the Old Man would appear for a short while. All the Mates would take a morning sun sight about 0900 in anticipation of a noon latitude sight.

There were 2 Radio Officers, and the junior would keep most of the watches. The senior did the Purser's work, but also did the relief's. The watches were related to which short wave radio station that they were in contact with. Very often this was Portishead in Somerset. They would also obtain regular time checks for the bridge to check off the chronometer.

A typical voyage would take you through the Suez Canal, down the Red Sea and to Aden. This was my first visit to the canal since the Suez War. There was some apprehension, as many seafarers were very concerned at the effects on standards and safety. It was the French who designed and built the canal, the Brits who financed and helped run it, via the Suez Canal Company. The Egyptians benefited through commerce, trade, employment, and there were many locals being trained and brought through the system. The nationalisation was

*Canal 8 ton scoop,
1957*

*Canal monument,
1957*

sheer political opportunism at a personal and internationally aided level. As it was, inexperienced and nervous Pilots, and managers, were thrust into the system.

Having said that, I used to love the transit. The arrival at Port Said, routines would be disrupted, but the hustle and bustle, the approved traders with their leather and touristy goods spread out on deck. The Gilly Gilly man with his tricks and pick pocket demonstrations. Mail from home, probably written the day after you sailed, but after 9 days away, very welcome. There was of course the anticipated thievery. You would wait for your allocated turn and then join the south bound convoy. Past the Johnny Walker sign, *'Born 1872 and still going strong'*, and into the canal. A steady speed, keeping your distance from the ship in front, sand banks either side, palm tree clumps, camels, donkeys, farmers and pedestrians going about their business, the hospital at Ismaelia within waving distance, and into the Bitter Lakes where you would anchor and wait for the north bound convoy. People would very often have a swim here. Sometimes you had to tie up in the canal to let the ships through. It would be very hot during the day, but at night it could be duffle coat cold. After a while you would rejoin the canal, sail past the canal widening crane, with its 8 ton scoop, which was one of the biggest in the world at the time, and onto Port Suez, drop the Pilot and into the Gulf of Suez.

The Red Sea would be very busy, and ships passed very close to each other. It's a surprise that there weren't more accidents. Cadets would very often use this at night for Morse lamp signalling practice. TTFNBV would end many a session. Ta ta for now, bon voyage. Three days to Aden. It would be very very hot, but also very windy, and if the wind was behind you, it could be uncomfortably airless. In the days before air conditioning and blowers, it was quite normal for a ship to make a complete circle to blow some fresh air through the accommodation. This is where the word POSH came from. Port

Jason foredeck in Sydney

Jason in Sydney Harbour

Out Starboard Home. Regular travellers on the P & O ships, a famous mail and passenger ship company, which ran to India and the Far East, would select their cabins on this basis, to avoid being on the sun side of the ship, which could be unbearable.

Aden worked 24/24. It hardly ever rained here, but on one occasion it actually did, and we had to stop cargo, which was unheard of. You took on bunkers, mail from home, and occasionally a little cargo. You left as quickly as possible. However, it was a cross roads, and with Japan emerging with some very good quality radios and binoculars, you could sometimes pick up a very good bargain from the Bumboats that were allowed alongside. They would throw up lines with small baskets; you would inspect the chosen goods, agree a price, either pay or return the items. There was much good natured haggling and noise. I bought a very good pair of binoculars here for £5.

The Indian Ocean could be very pleasant. Nine days or so to Fremantle. The swimming pool would be assembled on deck, and could be used by everybody, usually at agreed times. There would a gentle crossing of the line ceremony. Frantic games of deck tennis took place in the late afternoon before dinner. Also deck cricket. These were popular, and I was fit and athletic in those days.

Aussie was very popular, as the dockers would not work after 1800. This meant that you usually had at least 3 or 4 days in port, and very often 10 or 12. Work continued, but everybody had a chance to go ashore. Trips to the beaches, socialising, outdoor cinemas, see friends. The 2nd Mate was very keen on golf, so for the second voyage I acquired a second hand bunch of clubs. None from the same set, some with wooden shafts. Thanks to a donation from Uncle Bill. We had some great fun and played in Melbourne, Sydney and Adelaide.

The picture of the tug's smoke was taken at 0500 as we made our way up to Adelaide. It was a beautiful morning with a lovely background, and the smoke appeared as jet black.

*Jason dry-docked
in 1957*

"Is this my best side?"

Unfortunately it has not printed as clearly as the slide picture. Christmas on the first voyage was spent in Brisbane. Everything just closed down, but there was another company ship in port, so we celebrated together. We also dry-docked to have the hull painted. We were told that there would be a delay in pumping out when the dock was nearly empty. We soon realised why. When the water level was down to about four feet, the floor of the dock was covered in a silvery mass of wriggling fish of all types. None of us had ever seen anything like this before. The dock workers then proceeded to scoop this all up into baskets, and sold them to the assembled fishmongers. Eventually they returned to the work in hand.

We did manage two games of cricket against other ships. The one in Melbourne was abandoned when the new ball disintegrated due to the hardness of the wicket. I was 30 not out and we were on our way to victory. They have since built a giant sport stadium on the site to commemorate this feat. I was also able to visit the Taronga Park zoo in Sydney.

The instructions were to proceed to Portland, a small port south of Melbourne, but outside of the heads. You will be the first company and largest ship to go there. See how you get on. There was a wooden jetty that stuck out into the sea with a permanent heavy swell. There were large sprung wooden fenders, to soften the ship bouncing on to and up to 15 feet off. The gangway could not be landed on the quay. It was very hairy, but work started and proceeded steadily, albeit slowly. The local farmers did all the work, and there was a collection of curious sightseers on the quay the whole time. Families and locals. The State of Victoria stuck to the 1800 closing time. The message went round the ship that if we went to the local hotel and said that we were travellers, we would be alright. After dinner a large group of us solemnly proceeded through a typical Wild West town, with single track railway, a few shops, a few houses and a pub. We were met, asked to sign the visitors book, and we

Glasgow bump

Brussels World Fair 1958

truthfully stated that we had travelled down from Sydney, some 800 miles away. We were led to a back room. The place was set up for a party. The locals were in, the bar in full swing, the buffet ready, and the leader of the music group on the saxophone was the local Chief of Police. We had a wonderful evening. They were very friendly and hospitable. Later on in the voyage I was told that I would be joining another ship. Blue Flue did not like Junior Officers getting too comfy. The *Jason* was a happy ship.

There then followed a short period of coasting. Whilst in Glasgow we were able to observe the launching of a tanker, the *Hurricane*, from the other side of the river. She duly slipped down the slipway and kept coming, closer and closer. Eventually she hit the quay very close to us. We were all highly amused. Thankfully there was no damage or injury. When in Antwerp, some of us had the chance to visit the World Fair. Very impressive and futuristic.

Ajax

October 1958 to February 1959

The *Ajax* was on a normal Far East schedule, and this time She would be going to Japan. Almost a repeat of my first voyage on the *Ascanius*, even the same Old Man, Dougie Stroud. Hardly ever saw him, but he could be very droll. She was one of the newer A class boats, and was a nice ship. The voyage to Aden would be the same, but then it was due east to Malaya. On the way home we were diverted to Djibouti, a French North African port, because of political unrest in Aden. A sign of things to come.

The picture of Mt Fujiama was taken at sunrise, and it was very impressive. Unfortunately photos don't always do full justice.

China and Formosa (Taiwan), were still on a war footing, and

Mount Fuji at sunrise

Stromboli

Ajax bow

*Warplane,
Formosa Straight 1958*

we had to suspend huge Union Flags on each side of the ship, and one prominently on a hatch top. We were often buzzed, and you never knew what the identification and intentions would be. On more than one occasion, ships had radioed the Royal Navy in Hong Kong in alarm.

Returning home through the Medi we were going to Genoa. This took us through the Straits of Messina. It was a lovely morning, and you go quite close to the land, and past the volcanic Island of Stromboli. It is still active, and wisps of smoke were visible.

At the end of the voyage I had sufficient sea time to be able to study for my Ist Mates certificate. This was a three month course which I did in Liverpool, and thankfully passed first time. Dot was now firmly on the scene.

Whilst on the course you meet people from other companies. Shorter voyages were an attraction, so I became interested in Elder Dempsters - round voyages of 10 weeks or so to West Africa. Mainly from Liverpool, but similar coastal routes to Blue Funnel.

ELDER DEMPSTERS
Accra
July to December 1959

My job interview was at the Deck Officers Personnel Department on the 6th floor of India Buildings. This required a lot of navigational skill, because it was on the same floor as, but at the opposite end of the passage, to the Blue Funnel Department. It seemed strange to turn left instead of right. The interview went well, which I expected, as Blue Funnel trained officers were highly regarded, of course. We did discuss my pending wedding arrangements, and this was duly honoured.

You are instructed to join MV *Accra* as Extra Third Mate in Canada Dock. You will start on Senior Third Mate's pay.

This was an excellent appointment. The *Accra* was one of three mail boats. They operated a weekly service from the Liverpool landing stage to *Apapa*, which was the port of Lagos in Nigeria. Sail on Thursday, redock on Sunday three weeks later. Strict schedule applied, so you knew where you were and when. The other two ships were the *Apapa*, an almost identical sister ship to the *Accra*, and the much newer *Aureol*. The first two had grey hulls, white superstructure, and the company yellow funnel. They were very practical vessels. The *Aureol* was all white with the company yellow funnel, but was beautifully designed and known as the 'White Goddess'. She was the Flag Ship and very popular with passengers and crew, and highly regarded throughout the fleet. The three ships were happy and popular postings. They were all about 12,000 tons gross with a service speed of 15 knots. They carried 250/300 passengers. Working Officers did not fraternise with passengers. The rules were very strict, and observed. The Captain, Chief Engineer and Purser had designated tables with the passengers, and were expected to attend if responsibilities allowed. Not always a popular assignment, although some senior officers did enjoy it.

As Extra Third mate, my duties were the 4-8 watch and I was also responsible for the lifeboat stores. This meant checking all the stores in the boats, including dates and condition. This wasn't too onerous, as these were checked in Liverpool each time, and I didn't have to physically check every boat, as I had had to do on cargo ships. There were 8 lifeboats, with sufficient places to carry all on board. This was a requirement as a result of the *Titanic* disaster. There were also inflatable life rafts. The Chief Officer was in charge of the 4-8, and it was normal for the x3/o to assist him. He was the senior c/o in the company, also ex Blue Flue, and had been on the last British ship to leave Penang when the Japs were advancing. He told me that the most frightening moment of his life had been when a solitary Jap plane had attacked, and they watched this single bomb as it fell towards them, but thankfully missed. We got on well. My Stand By position was on the Bridge with the Captain. This made sense as we usually sailed or docked in that watch.

There was no Officers bar in those days, so watchkeepers didn't have much socialising at sea. If you wanted a drink, usually ice cold draught lager, you rang a bell and the Officers Steward would attend to you. No cash involved, you signed a chit and it appeared on your account. The Chief Steward could keep an eye on this, and inform the Captain if there was any excessive imbibing. Health, and of course safety. There was no air conditioning, just warm air being pumped through the ventilation ducts. All Officers used a restaurant on the Boat Deck. This was OK for us, as it was only a few yards away. Bit of a pain for the Engineers, as their cabins were a long way away, but of course they did benefit from our company. Being a passenger ship, the food was excellent and varied, but was transported up to us by a rope lift direct to the galley. Steward service of course. The ship had its own bakery and printer. There was a daily newspaper, printed from the World service, as obtained by the Radio Officer. Headlines mainly, but also a very comprehensive stock market update. This was civilised living. There was a surgery with a doctor or surgeon, and a couple of nurses. Passengers had to pay privately, but the crew were treated under the NHS. The doctor was a very skinny, scrawny guy, who had been a POW with the Japs. He was a great character. He entertained well, he would get the husbands drunk on G & T, and would then attend to the needs of the wives. We knew it went on, they loved him.

The top two photos show the Bridge and accommodation taken by me from the cross trees on the foremast. Judging from the two watchkeepers it was a quiet moment. A time to appreciate the environment, and allow the luxury of a few thoughts of home. The prime duty of a watchkeeper was to keep a good lookout, and safety. Being a passenger ship, there was also a fire consol on the bridge, which was checked regularly. This worked by air being sucked out from the chosen compartments, including the passenger cabins, and a whiff of smoke would indicate a problem. Fire was the biggest fear of seafarers. No luxury of a 999 call, no space to get people out of the way for safety. We were the fire brigade, and all crew attended a short fire course. But firefighting was not our main job.

On top of the wheelhouse is an area with a brown wood surround. This was known as the Monkey Island. A very important place, which was kept clear of unnecessary goods. In it are three pieces of equipment. The forward one, the one with two spheres on, is the master magnetic compass. This is the pivot of the ship's navigation, but being magnetic, it can be affected by metal objects nearby, including wristwatches. The Earth is a giant magnet, but the magnetic pole is a long way away from the North Pole. Also the Earth's magnetic field varies in direction and strength in different parts of the world. The ship is a giant magnetic bar, and the effect on the compass is changed by what course she is on. These errors are known about, and there are navigational tables about them, but they have their limitations. Error checks are done every watch, and after each alter course, and are recorded. This can be very useful on later voyages, if up-to-date checks aren't possible, due to weather or other priorities.

The middle piece, with the grey cover, is a Giro repeater. This is also error checked and compared with the magnetic. It is also checked at each watch change against the steering repeater, and also the master giro, which is housed elsewhere, often in the bowels of the ship. The giro is a mechanical machine, and errors can creep in due to dust, grease, oil, vibration, power surges, temperature etc. Virtually everything that is normal for shipboard life. There is also another magnetic compass in the wheelhouse as a reserve steering compass. These readings are recorded in the log. One had to expect that the giro could go off at any time, without warning, and one was prepared. Thankfully it didn't happen too often, but one developed the habit of checking the two compasses every time one went by. In the days of helmsmen they would alert you if strange things started to happen, if they were awake. Two hours on the wheel, even one, if you are tired, or drunk, can be hypnotic. The Watchkeeping Officer had to keep an eye on these things, even if he was also 'dead on his feet'.

The third item, the white lollipop, is the radio direction finder. Not used very often now, but was required by law, a legacy from the war. It could be used to help track weak radio signals from a lifeboat, and occasionally as a navigational back up.

My Stand By duties would be to attend to the telegraph instructions. Make sure that they had been acted on properly. Keep a log of all engine movements, and special situations, make sure that the helmsman repeated and acted on his instructions, attend to VHF and flag signals, and keep the ship's position up-to-date on the chart. Cups of tea for the Pilot and Old Man. Once tied up, or anchored, finish the log, and then go ashore to read the draft. If at anchor, I had to use a boat. Usually the Agent's launch. I was the only person allowed off the ship before Customs and Immigration had finished. Before sailing I had to read the draft, enter it on the draft sheet, get the C/o and Captain to sign it, and return it to its displayed position. This was a legal requirement. Mr Plimsoll and all that.

Because of the schedules, the *Accra* and *Aureol* would pass very close to each other in Freetown harbour, as one ship took the berth that the other had vacated. On a few occasions when John was travelling, we were able to pick each other out and give a wave.

Cargo work was fairly easy. We carried lots of mailbags, well sorted out and separated. We also carried a lot of 'specie', small, but heavy boxes of coins. It was the run up to independence of a number of the countries, and they were changing the currency. There was a special locker in No. 3 hatch, which was well secured, we even had to put lead seals on the padlocks. These were checked every day. The rest of the cargo would be light general, with passenger baggage the bulk. Homeward bound we would sometimes pick up small bananas from Takoradi, and small tomatoes from Las Palmas. Depended on the season.

The schedule would be to arrive at Las Palmas 0600, take on oil, very little cargo, and sail 1600. Personal mail was always welcome. Similar for Freetown and Takoradi, although we would sail later, as there would have been passengers disembarking, or joining, but no oiling. Arrival at *Apapa* was more relaxing, as when the passengers were gone we had a few days of relative normal routine as watches would be broken. There wasn't much to do ashore, although of course I knew Jim and Dorothy Payne. He was the Mission to Seamen Padre that I had met in Liverpool, through an introduction from my cousin Paul Britton. We still keep in touch.

The Agent in Gran Canary sometimes arranged a couple of mini buses to take some passengers on a sight seeing tour of the Island. This was a whistle stop affair, but on one occasion there were a couple of spare seats, and the Captain invited off duty officers if they would like to go. I was luckily one of them. This was a time well before tourism took off, although some wealthy people had started to buy second homes in Las Palmas. One photo shows a very attractive garden that we passed, and two are general scenes of the hills and the extinct volcano. At the bottom of this is a farm and golf course. Very dramatic and awe inspiring.

There is the entrance to the river at Lagos. It looks serene, but in fact hides a very fast flowing current. When departing, you would feel the ship lifting and moving to the swell before you cleared the breakwater. In the distance you can see the back of the sheds of *Apapa* wharf, where most ships tied up and worked. This was a new dock area and could accommodate over 20 ships. It was also subject to the strong current, and there was a horrible tragedy next to the *Accra*. It was a Sunday afternoon, the ship was loading some cargo from a company coaster which was tied up alongside. A quiet routine scene. A small motor boat was passing with three adults and a dog on board. They recognised some friends on board and came closer to exchange greetings. They couldn't hear, so turned the engine down. Unfortunately it cut out, the current caught the boat, swept it between the two ships and forced one end down. Luckily there were a number of people around, and ropes and a rope ladder were quickly lowered. Two adults and the dog were rescued, but the other adult went into the cabin to get something, and was not seen again. I will never forget the look on the face of his young widow, who came down to the scene a couple of hours later. She, and members of the crew, just could not believe that something like that could happen on a quiet, routine, sunny afternoon - a vivid reminder of the forces of nature. He was found a few days later. She, and the kids were flown home on the next available flight. Danger and seafaring are close companions. You learn to live with, acknowledge, and respect the elements. Unfortunately, modern attitudes seem to think that they know it all, and totally disregard this.

There are two photos at sea. One, a lovely day, a little wind, but a moderate swell developing. The bow of the *Accra* was quite high, and you didn't often have spray as heavy as this. It may look fluffy, but could knock a man over. People were not allowed on the foredeck those days.

Sunset, homeward bound. Many sunsets in the tropics could be absolutely beautiful. Indescribable. Often a photo would only show a yellow blob on a dark background. This picture does capture some of the beauty. Sunset and sunrise usually

Accra spray

*Sunset
1959*

*Accra
bridge*

happened in the 4-8. A bonus. The structure on the right is a Bridge wing shelter, which is for the protection of the Captain and Pilot when docking the ship in heavy torrential tropical rain. Also to keep me dry when they were not around.

One of the biggest benefits of my time on the *Accra*, was the duty free that I was able to build up over a number of short voyages. A bottle of spirits, and one wine each voyage. This was very much appreciated by Dot's family at our wedding. There was none left when we returned from our honeymoon. Also the short time in Liverpool between voyages, meant that I was able to build up some leave, which covered the wedding, and a week's honeymoon, with a few days over.

After the *Accra* I did a short period of coasting on other ships until 21 Feb 1960. This involved relieving the deep sea crew for their leave whilst their ship was being discharged, and loaded, around the UK and continent. This could include drydocking and surveys. Sometimes the company would charter a Dakota to take a crew from Liverpool International Airport to Amsterdam Schipol Airport.

Sulima

March – October 1960

The wedding was booked for 5th March. We had no indication of my next ship, but we did have enough leave for at least one week's honeymoon, which had been duly arranged at the Metropole Hotel in Blackpool. The big day was a great success and a very happy occasion. The hotel was owned by Butlins, but did specialise in honeymoons, and had been recommended to us. We had a wonderful time. Whilst away, I did phone the company, and was given the name of my next ship, an approximate date for joining, and that I would be promoted to Extra 2nd Mate. This was good news, and meant that we could have another week away, which we took. But there was a sting in the tail.

On reporting to the Office, I was told that the Sulima was the company African Cadet Ship, that the Chief Officer did not keep a watch. Hence the extra officer. There was a good chance that she would be going to America. Everyone had to take their turn. The voyage would probably take over six months. Welcome back Tony, tuff luck Dot.

The company operated two cadet ships. One African, one British. These were intended to give practical experience of the running of a ship for cadets. This meant doing everything that a sailor could be asked to do. Most people who went on them found them to be hard work, good fun, but a very rewarding experience. MN rules required that they had at least 5 certificated Able Bodied Seamen (AB's), on board. There were minimum manning rules for different duties. Most of the cadets were Nigerian. It was the time of Independence, and they were full of it. Nigerians can be excitable at the best of times.

The senior 2nd mate would keep the 4-8 watch and look after the practical cargo work. He had a Masters certificate and was an excellent person to work with. I kept the 12-4, and was responsible for the navigation. Mac was the Third officer, and did the 8-12 watch, as well as the safety equipment. He was from Freetown in Sierra Leone, over 6 foot tall, and a terrific man. The cadets were in awe of him, and he could say things that we couldn't. We all got on very well with each other. A quiet little word in the right ear helped sort out a few problems. We usually found that the Ghanaian and Freetown men to be very good to work with, but that the Nigerians could be argumentative, even amongst themselves.

Nigeria had three dominant tribes. The Hausa in the north, who were mainly Muslim. They were a very proud and honourable group then. Uncle John was a District Commissioner there for many years. A devout Christian, he had a good relationship with them. They formed the backbone of the Army. Afraid that has all changed now, as the fundamentalists have taken over, and some horrible things have happened, including large scale Christian massacres. They did keep out of the later Biafran war. This involved the Eboe and Youraba tribes. The Eboes tended to be in Western Nigeria, the townies around Lagos, the business, commercial, political communities. The Youraba were the Niger delta people, mainly fishermen and agricultural, very poor, and well spread out. That is where the oil deposits were found. Enough said. They hated each other, and there were some horrible atrocities. The going rate for an enemy's head was £50. Lovely people.

We sailed from Liverpool and did a normal run down the West African coast, discharging general cargo, which included: cars, booze, pipes, cement, buckets, spades, bibles, machinery etc. Freetown was first, where we picked up our Kroo boys. These were a gang of twenty or thirty auxiliary sailors, who stayed with us on the coast. They brought their own food, utensils, and bedding. They were given a cargo hatch tent, which they would rig up on a hatch top or deck, as desired, and also access to water for their comfort. They worked hard, and seemed quite happy, and it wasn't unusual for them to occasionally sing hymns and have bible readings when work quietened down. Then we sailed to Takoradi and then to *Apapa*, the port of Lagos. During this time, it was confirmed that we were going to do the American run. All the Brits were thrilled. There was already tension starting on board, it was very hot, sticky, uncomfortable, hard work, long hours, and no air conditioning. The Nigerians were full of Independence, but, surprisingly, when you spoke to the ordinary docker or tally clerk, who could all speak very good English, most of them were very apprehensive and sad to see the Brits go. We were already training our replacements, and the companies were subsidising and creating fleets to take over

Jim's garden

Lagos locals

Sulima cargo

from them. With the benefit of hindsight, can anybody claim that the ideal and concept of Independence has been a success for the general population in West Africa. The chosen few, and Swiss bank accounts maybe, but what about the ordinary people. The locals, and ex-pats, all said at the time, that it was rushed through and ill thought out. But, of course, the politicians and civil servants in London, they know best. Stability, law, order, education, communication, health, government, all take time to establish. Plans were already in hand.

We retraced our steps along the coast, loading logs, bales of rubber, bags of cocoa, and 60 green monkeys for Canada and USA. These were in cages on deck, and looked after by the sailors. They were paid extra for this, and became very fond of them. Green monkeys later became linked to the spread of HIV. I don't know if this was ever proved.

When we first arrived in Montreal, work had ended for the day, most of the officers and crew went ashore, but it was my turn to keep ship. For safety reasons, a minimum number of designated crew had to be on board at all times. The sailors got into party mode, but, unfortunately a green monkey escaped. I don't know how, but there it was halfway out on the topping lift wires of a derrick. These are the horizontal wires which hold the derrick top up. This was when I became aware of the situation. The 2nd Bosun shot up the Samson post and he started to clamber onto the wires. Thirty to forty feet above the deck. Now these are very greasy, and designed to twist when weight was applied to them. I remonstrated with him and asked him to come down. He assured me that his family had a circus background and continued in pursuit. The monkey thought that this was great fun, and when his keeper got closer, duly hopped off the end of the derrick, which was conveniently only a few feet from the edge of the very large flat roof of the warehouse. His pursuer eventually followed, thankfully still in one piece. There then ensued an exciting chase, with a number of helpers, with eventual success. By this time, those still on board were all in hysterics. What if the monkey had escaped, or he had slipped? Then there would have been trouble, big trouble. An International Immigration and safety incident. But is life about 'what ifs'? It didn't happen. The officer on duty had sorted it out. Of course. Pass the tin opener, no pull tags then.

The Captain was a Pole. He had been on destroyers during the war, possibly in command, and was an absolute charmer. He had been Chief Officer on the Flagship *Aureol* for some time, and had a big reputation with the ladies. On more than one occasion, as we sailed up through the creeks, we would suddenly come to a small clearing with a large brick house, and there would be a scantily clad female running down the garden waving to him. Unfortunately he kept himself remote from the day to day running of the ship, as Captain's did then, and an undercurrent of problems started to build up. One of these surfaced in Montreal later on. The initial rush to get cargo discharging was over, and we settled into a steady port routine. Watches had been broken, and we took it in turns to man the deck. Day work only. A time to catch up on mail, laundry etc. The *Saxonia*, a Cunard medium sized passenger ship had docked nearby, and the officers had issued an invitation to us, through the agent, to go and visit them. Our Captain and Chief Officer thought this was a good idea. An opportunity to see how the other half lived. This was arranged, and the Chief Officer would look after the ship. We were shown around, it was very interesting, and we were very impressed with the size and difference of routines and priorities. We duly ended up in one of our host's cabins. The hospitality and comradeship of the sea took over, and it was dinner before we returned to our home base. We were very happy, it was the first time that we had had time off together, and there had been tensions that we had shared. C/O was not impressed. He thought we would be away for a couple of hours, and had missed his kip. We were summoned to the Captain's cabin next morning. Mutiny, dereliction of duty, abandoning ship, safety at sea, licence cancellation were bandied about. It was going to be very grave. Actually the Old Man was embarrassed, realised what had happened, but had to support the C/O. So we had a stern lecture, and had to promise that it wouldn't happen again. This we reluctantly did. Actually, there was no chance that that sort of circumstance could ever happen again. Later the Captain was very glad of my loyalty, when we were leaving our last port of Freetown homeward bound.

Occasionally at sea there would be special 'one off' events. It was decided that the cadets should be taken on a tour of the city. The 3/0 and I would lead them, in uniform. It was very interesting and enjoyable, despite the fact that on a couple of occasions, as the only white man in the group, I was hissed at. Political correctness and ignorance go hand in hand. However, the one or two people who did actually speak to me, were impressed with what we were doing. Mind you, I did have my revolver, fixed bayonet, ankle shackles, and bullwhip, swinging from my belt at the time. I hadn't shaved, and my cutlass was dragging on the floor. It was of course my off duty and rest time.

The Canadians were very proud of the new St Lawrence Seaway. We were shown the main road bridge over the St Lawrence River. This had been raised 25 feet, an inch at a time, without stopping the traffic. This was a major engineering feat, and enabled the joining of the sea, river and inland waterways. We were also shown the huge empty Winter pits where they dumped the snow. 3 million tons of it. The roads are very rarely closed in winter. The last call was the Red Indian reserve. The Red Indians duly did their touristy bit. Very exciting, and I did save the cost of a haircut. Mind you, the cadets were holding me down at the time, but then the Red Coats arrived. Aren't they wonderful?

We sailed for New York down the Seaway. Beautiful scenery, and my first view of the Aurora Borealis. We docked next to the

Montreal

Seaway Lock

New York from berth

Brooklyn Bridge, and were told that we would be loading flour. Thousands of tons of the stuff. The picture shows the view from our berth.

This meant a full fumigation. The Yanks are very strict about this. The ship is closed down and the crew evacuated to a nearby hotel. A skeleton crew, comprising a deck and engineer officer, and a couple of sailors, remain on the dock, and are allocated an office to rest. The two chemists then board the ship and set off their canisters of cyanide gas in every compartment. A watchman is stationed at the bottom of the gangway. A ghost ship for 36 hours. I was on duty when the chemists decided to re-enter the ship. All compartments were visited, but on entering a hatch compartment, the front chemist suddenly turned round, held his breath, and I was told to get out, quick. On deck we took deep breaths, we could smell almonds, and it was decided that the ship wasn't ready. We then went off for my first American breakfast. Two eggs sunny side up. Later the ship was declared safe, we reboarded, started up the machinery, and next morning commenced loading bags of flour.

We then sailed to Norfolk and Baltimore to finish off. We had a bit of time off in Baltimore, and it was going to be our last opportunity ashore for some time. The senior officers, and those without responsibilities, were going to go up town and paint it red. Taxis, nite clubs, whatever. Three of us, newly weds or saving, with modest means, decided to stay local. Chats with stevedores established that a very good short cut to a street with some bars, was via a very long tubular grain passageway that we could see, high above the ground. You will be alright they said. We entered the tower and climbed the vertical ladders to the passage. It was a very long walk. Then we became aware of the rats. The biggest that I have ever seen. Cat size. We also realised that we hadn't brought a torch for the home journey. At the end we soon discovered the street, it was early, so we decided to do a reccy, have a drink in each bar, and then go

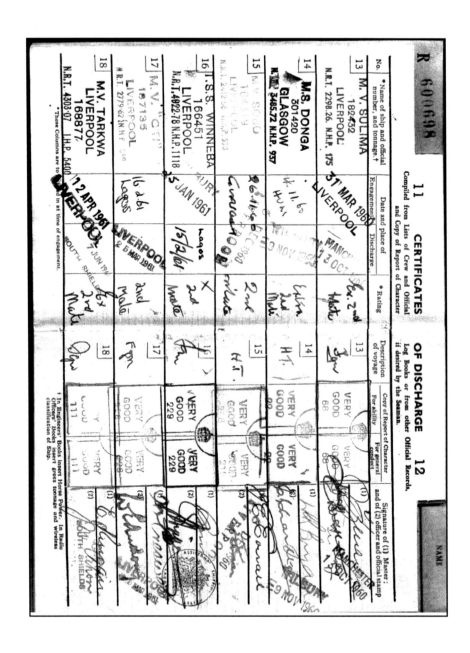

back to the one that we liked. This we did. American draught lager served in plastic cups slightly less than a half pint. By this time some locals had started to surface, as soon as they realised that we were Brits, they sent us round after round down to us. 'No thanks' was not understood, it was embarrassing, but a wonderful night. Very hospitable. Our end of the bar was smothered with full cups. Eventually we couldn't take any more, and headed back. Rats, what rats. They heard us, they disappeared, but we did have a lighter to guide us home, and we could see their eyes. Not a place to fall down. We were first back about midnight. At breakfast we met the others. It had been a disaster, a rip off. The taxi was expensive, the niteclubs were pathetic and expensive, the meals very ordinary. They did not appreciate our experience, which had cost us about 10 bob each. They were not happy. We were, and happily shared our experiences. Eventually we loaded up, and sailed back across the Atlantic. There was an atmosphere.

On our return to the West Coast, we solemnly discharged the flour, as shown in the picture. This was a very popular cargo with the dockers. The white powder from burst bags was considered to be very cosmetic, and the smaller white bags were highly sort out as tea shirts and singlets. The bright printing made them irresistible. Thankfully, we were told that on completion, we would be loading for home, Manchester.

In Takoradi we were moored to the buoys for a few days, loading logs directly from the water. Some of them weighed up to 15 tons. We were working around the clock. The *Obuasi*, the British Cadet ship, came in and berthed alongside the wharf. She was discharging outward bound. The company normally tried to keep the two ships apart, but this was not always possible. We didn't think anything of this, and carried on working normally. She was on the other side of the harbour, and a long way away. One morning there was holy hell on. A boarding party had visited us during the night, painted a very large 'N' in white, on our pristine yellow funnel, which had only just been painted for home and Head Office. 'N' was the symbol on the funnel for the new Nigerian National Line. Black on a green and black background. Some of us thought that this was highly amusing, and admired the skill and courage of the prank. Others saw it as a diplomatic and international incident, an insult, irresponsible and highly dangerous. Signals were exchanged between the two Captains, and eventually a working party came over and repainted our funnel. There was an atmosphere. I later sailed with the ringleader when he was Chief Officer on the *El Brega*. A great character, he was fearless and very professional.

Occasionally the mail got out of synch. Unfortunately, this was one of those instances. My mail got hopelessly out of order. From the dates, I knew that there was a big gap. Dot started talking about seeing the Doctor, again. I had no inkling as to why, although a sinking feeling did start to develop. Eventually, when we were in the creeks, very sticky, very uncomfortable, very fed up, all was revealed. She was expecting. Goodbye honeymoon, hello parenthood. At the end of the voyage, we had been married for 7 ½ months, she was 7 months pregnant, and we had been together for just over 3 weeks.

At last it was Freetown. Last port, fully loaded, and homeward bound. We were at anchor, finishing loading from one lighter, it was slow and after midnight. Being 12-4 I was on duty, and everybody was turned in, as sea watches had continued. The Old Man had been entertaining the Agent and his wife. They had had a good time. When completion of cargo was imminent, I told him, and proceeded with seagoing preparations. The visitors left, and the C/O went forward with the Carpenter to start heaving up the anchor. The foredeck was covered with logs, which were wet and slippery, and unfortunately the forward phone was out of action. So we had to rely on the megaphone. I was on the Bridge with the Duty Cadet. When an anchor is being heaved up, the bell is struck which indicates how many shackles of cable are still out. A shackle is a length of cable 15 fathoms long, 90 feet. Near each join, a link is marked with white paint and some wire, which indicates what number that section is. My call to the Captain was unanswered, so I sent the Cadet down to tell him. When he returned the anchor away signal, a rapid ringing of the focs'le bell, was being given just as he was telling me that he could not rouse the Old Man. I was in charge. I rang the telegraph for slow ahead, and steered to avoid other anchored ships. We bellowed for the C/O to come to the bridge. This of course took some time, but instead of going straight there, he went to the Captain's cabin. This took more time. By now we were well on our way out. Eventually the two senior men appeared on the bridge and I was solemnly given the course to steer from the Fairway buoy. This is the last buoy to a navigation channel near a harbour. This was of course the course that as navigator, I had set down. I was rather amused. There was an awkward atmosphere after that, but I was very pleased with my effort as stand-in Captain and Pilot.

Eventually we arrived at the Ship Canal and tied up for the night, to await our turn for the passage. It was a drizzly autumnal evening, the nearest red phone box was nearly a mile away, and I had to estimate, and wait, for when my Father-in-Law was likely to be in the Allerton. Eventually contact was made, and I was able to tell him that I was home. The passage was interesting, and arrangements were made for Dot to join me for a couple of days before I left the ship. Not one of my happiest voyages.

The Chief Officer had come under the influence of the Bosun, and they kept themselves to themselves, and were not popular. The Bosun was a big man, and a bit of a bully. This created problems later.

The sailors were young and in their early twenties. They had a bad reputation and double D.R's in their Discharge books. In practice, when you got to know them, you could talk to them, and they were very good workers. But, when they hit the pop, they went over the top. As we saw later on. Every seaman has a Discharge book. It is more important than a Passport, which none of us had. When you signed on, the ship's stamp and date were entered. There was space for dates, Captain's signature and conduct stamps. Usually VG, Very Good. A very bad disciplinary record resulted in D.R's. This meant that you were virtually unemployable. Except of course, on African Cadet Ships.

On the final leg home, the sailors did gang up on the Bosun and beat him up. No action was taken.

In view of my changed circumstances, the company were very good to us. After 3 weeks leave at home, I did some short relieving voyages, which meant that I would be home over Christmas and the eagerly anticipated event.

This was actually a very lovely and happy time. Hello Susan.

After that I did 2 more 2-month voyages, before swallowing the anchor.

Merchant seamen were exempt from National Service up to the age of 26. When this ended, it did open the door to go ashore. Unfortunately there weren't many opportunities for our type of experience, but selling insurance was one. I joined the National Mutual Life Association of Australasia Ltd, based in Liverpool, and worked the ships in the docks for 6 years. This meant calling on the Officers, and trying to persuade them to take out life assurance. It was stressful, hard, but I did have success, made a lot of friends, and we did have a lot of fun. We did start to buy our own house. My ambition had always been to create a happy settled home.

PART TWO

My Return to Sea

Age 38-43

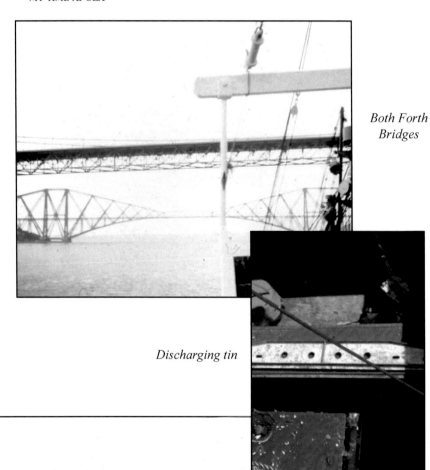

*Both Forth
Bridges*

Discharging tin

*River Elbe
entrance*

Ocean Fleets

In all, I spent 14 years ashore. June 1961 – July 1975. But as the Merchant Navy declined, business became harder. We moved to Shrewsbury so that I could join a firm of Insurance Brokers, the best decision we ever made. A very happy time, but income expectations and a wage freeze meant that it became financially unviable.

In the meantime, I had been approached by my old manager in Liverpool, Jim Anderton, to join a new, but forward looking, company, Abbey Life. This I did, self-employed, but 6 very exciting, highly pressured years followed. Working from home, I covered Shropshire, but went to Liverpool every week to attend training and branch meetings. Although we were working on our own, very lonely sometimes, and in some senses were in competition with each other, a tremendous spirit of encouragement and support was built up. Visits to Majorca, great social occasions, and the prize of dreams, 5 days in Bermuda. Unsocial hours, stress, but it is the good times that one remembers. Unfortunately a change of Government brought in the Socialists. Recession, collapse of confidence in investments, shares, commercial property. Unemployment soared. This included a political attack on small businesses and the self-employed. We were introduced to inflation of 26%, mortgage interest rates of 15%, savings of 10%. Council 'rates'/tax rocketed. The IMF was forced to step in, and things did start to settle down slowly. There was virtually no help for parents, although we did qualify briefly for a very small reduction in rates. This was financially unsustainable. In the meantime, the MN had started to advertise for officers to return to sea. A number started to drift back, and I duly joined them.

One of my options was Ocean Fleets. Blue Funnel and Elder Dempsters had merged with a couple of other companies and were also involved with the new container ships. My interview was in the same office in India buildings that I had left 14 years ago, where I had been solemnly told that I would never get a job with Blue Funnel again. The manager who told me that, subsequently became janitor of India Buildings. Ah well. The new manager, Mr Felice, was very friendly, very keen to have me back, and happily gave me my old seniority. There was of course a manning shortage.

My priority was always to keep the family together and a roof over our heads. We were not better off financially, but the income was regular, seniority and promotion soon took over. It was a very very hard decision to take, but the family were growing up, and they were very strong together. But I hated being away. That was very difficult. The marriages of some of my ex colleagues did in fact break up. Things had changed.

However, I did have to re-register with the Shipping Federation in Liverpool, and this went through on 3rd July 1975. The company also insisted that I attended a radar refresher course. An instrument that I had always found to be interesting. Later I did a 5 day MN fire course in Edinburgh. This involved a lot of breathing apparatus work, including accommodation fires and a simulated engine room fire where you had to walk above flames. Not to be recommended. It was very intense, and very uncomfortable. But I was able to have a quick look around the city.

I was appointed to the M.V. *Laomedon* as an Extra 2nd Mate, for coastal duties. On 12th July 1975 the relieving crew assembled at Liverpool Speke Airport to join a chartered Dakota, which would fly us to Schipol Airport near Amsterdam. A bumpy and not very comfortable ride, but we got there This was new to me, although I had flown before. No more long boring train and ferry journeys. On board the duties were light, and I was allowed to reacclimatise myself. It soon came back, this was a class of ship that I had sailed on many times. We sailed for Hull, and I was an extra watchkeeper. This was a useful warm-up. The deep sea crew left, and I kept the 8-12 on the run round Scotland to Liverpool. In the past, this would have meant double watches, ie. two Officers on at the same time, and the Captain not far away. I was on my own, and we soon sailed into thick fog. As per instructions, I called the Old Man, he came up, had a quick look around, said I was OK and went back down. I was on my own. In view of my rustiness, this surprised, but appealed to me, and I enjoyed the challenge. The deep sea crowd rejoined there. There then followed 6 months of coasting. Short 2-3 weeks voyages around the UK and Continent with generous periods of leave in between. Very enjoyable, and time to be shared with the family.

Automedon

02 January – 16 March 1976

On the 2nd of January 1976, I flew out to join the *Automedon* in Hamburg to do my first deep sea voyage since rejoining. The crew were Chinese from Hong Kong, with a young and very good bosun. The ship was under charter to the Nigerian National Line, one of the companies set up by Elder Dempsters as part of Independence. The funnel was painted with that company's livery. We were immediately hit by one of the strongest storms ever with winds over 100 miles/hour. There was much structural damage in Europe, including tiles at home. Poor Dot had to cope with this. Very high floods soon followed, and soon the wharves were under feet of water. Stacks of containers were toppled and floated off into the river. The water filled the bottom of railway trucks. Work of course stopped, but we had to start watches to keep an eye on the mooring ropes. These just disappeared into the water, we could not see the ends. The Supercargo, an officer appointed to help us liaise with the European stevedores, was a Dutchman, he just shook his head and said, these German's will never learn, as soon as you build flood walls, you lift the height of the water.   When cargo did resume, we then had to stop whilst the authorities removed an unexploded wartime bomb nearby. Apparently this was a regular occurrence. When we left, we were fully loaded, and had a few thousand tons of German lager for Nigeria for a Government celebration. This did mean that we were a priority ship. Very important. It was the time of the infamous cement ships. A politician had made a miscalculation, and there were over 800 ships at anchor outside Lagos loaded with cement. We duly joined them. Some of the foreign flag ships had been there over 18 months, and were desperate. No stores, no mail, no water. To survive, they had to catch their own fish and water. It was distressing to listen to them on the VHF when we were on watch at night. The radar screen was just a mass of dots. If you can imagine an area from Shrewsbury to Oswestry 3 miles wide. There were also pirate raids, with many running battles on ships' decks. We escaped this, as we were well out. But the Captain of a Danish ship was killed on his bridge not far away.

After a few days, we were called in to *Apapa* to replace a sister ship. The Captain had been forced to sail at the point of a gun, even though they had not finished discharging. Whilst we had been at anchor, the President had been shot in a coup. We were apprehensive. Because of horrific congestion, the docks were closed at 6 pm, and the dockers were expected to do 24 hours non stop. The poor chaps were zombies, and of course became dangerous due to fatigue. So much for Independence. We were discharging the lager straight onto the lorries, which of course became popular focal points for the armed police and soldiers, who all wanted their share of the goodies. Tempers flared, and a few shots were loosed. Nobody got hit, but one avoided looking over the side, unless one had to. The 2 mini buses that Blue Peter had arranged a couple of years before, were still there, less wheels, batteries etc. We were alongside for 10 days, and the Chinese thought the Nigerians were a huge joke. We were glad to leave. It was the time of Chinese New Year. Traditionally the sailors would invite all officers for a meal that they had prepared, usually in the open on deck, and the hospitality would be very generous. Usually whisky. One had to bear in mind one's watchkeeping duties. The party would last for a couple of hours, when the sailors would be left to enjoy themselves. A blind eye would then be turned for their big session. We loaded up for Glasgow. We had been away 10 weeks. A spell of leave followed, and then some more coasting.

Ebani

28 April -18 July 1976

Proceed to King George V dock in Glasgow, you will be loading a lot of whisky which will be in open stow for West Africa. You will be 2nd Mate, but there will be an extra junior watchkeeper because of this. Usually spirits are stowed in special secure lockers, and kept under very tight surveillance.

On arrival I found that the dock had changed a lot, see picture, but that the work was quiet and steady. The extra third mate was a very mild Hindu and had his wife with him to do the voyage. A lovely couple. The Old Man then joined. An extrovert, who soon made his presence heard. We were told that the whisky would soon be loaded, that we were not to worry about it, as it only cost 7/6d (75p) a bottle, with most of the

King George V Glasgow dock

Accra canoes

*Lome
mending nets*

value being made up by tax, and that we weren't to take risks in saving it. In the meantime, the extra mate decided that he couldn't cope with all this, and signed off. It was too late for a replacement. The *Ebani* was one of 4 ships that carried up to 11 passengers, and they duly boarded, 3 couples and 4 single elderly ladies. Being on the 12/4, I didn't have a lot to do with them, although everybody would meet up for pre-dinner drinks. Being one of the older persons on board I got on quite well with them, and it was a change not to talk about ships all the time. The Captain had visions of being a grand socialiser. The 12/4 became a safe haven.

We started discharging in Freetown, without problems, and then to Takoradi. Freetown was usually a popular place to visit, you rarely went ashore, but the people were very friendly and good workers, and the first mail from home. Next time there, we would be on our way home.

Takoradi was the main port for Ghana. Ghana was now independent under Dr Nkrumah, who had very close ties with the Russian communists. In fact they created a second special port for the Russian fishing fleets at Sekondi which was nearby. Not as friendly as it used to be, and the work suffered. However, there was a Seafarers Mission Padre there, and he was very active. We were able to supply him with items which he couldn't get hold of, including chemicals for the swimming pool, which was a disgusting green with algae, and other nasties. We were able to use this on our way home. He did arrange a mini bus for the passengers and off duty officers to visit the Lion beach. Luckily I was able to join them. This had been a top class resort, but sadly was now very neglected. The buildings and facilities were not open, there were cracks in the brickwork, and the paint was decayed and peeling. But the sand was superb, and you could see why it had been so popular. Hopefully the photos show this. It was named after an offshore rock formation.

*Mission pool,
Takoradi*

Apapa wharf

Takoradi docks

Next port, Lome, the main access to Togoland, a very poor and small country. This was going to be very different. There was just the one wharf, and we had over 1,500 tons of steel plates to discharge. These weighed between 1 to 5 tons each. The facilities were very basic, and the discharging was very slow and very noisy, and round the clock. We split the day, and being the senior, I had to do 1830-0630. This lasted for 3 weeks, non-stop. Sleep time was in the morning and afternoon. My cabin was on a working alleyway, where officials would visit the Captain and Chief Officer. The biggest hatch was outside my cabin window. Metal bashing into metal, bang, bang, bang. It was very tiring, and took its toll. In the meantime the whisky was still being pilfered, and my colleague actually had a revolver pulled on him by a policeman, who wanted his share. What we did was to turn it into a bit of a game. We would search and frisk the dockers as they came out of the hatches, and confiscate when we were successful. But we would miss the occasional one. They soon cottoned on, and it became a bit of fun and joke. We survived. We finished discharging after midnight, and immediately set sail for Cotonou. It was only a short run and here we anchored.

We went alongside in the morning, a small jetty sticking out into the sea. The main port to Benin. Another small very poor country. Things were a lot quieter, but we still had whisky on board. I was able to have a wander on the beach, which is where I took the photo of the fishermen tending their nets. We finished discharging after midnight, and proceeded to Douala in the Cameroons. Not an easy place to find. A very broad estuary with no distinguishing features, and where the buoyage system was known to shift. We arrived safely, and started to load for home. Mainly logs from the water. Always a welcome time.

We also went to Tema. This was a new modern port constructed to replace *Accra*. *Accra* had been the first port for Ghana, but you had to anchor offshore. There was always a swell, the ship would roll steadily, and it was quite dangerous to work cargo. This would be transported in the canoes, see photo, which required a tremendous amount of skill and courage to work. Note the pronged paddles to ward off the evil sea spirits. Very effective too.

We anchored for a couple of days, as we waited our turn to go alongside, but we kept our seagoing watches going as this was an area noted for pirates. A time of quiet, and opportunity to catch up on navigation paperwork, including chart corrections. On the second night, it was lovely and peaceful, I had been working steadily, it was about 0200, and I decided to stretch my legs and wandered to the front of the bridge compartment. The window was open and as I leant on it, I became aware of 2 canoes alongside, with men clambering up the ship's side. They shouldn't be there. Without thinking, I bellowed at them. The full bellow. Luckily I caught them off balance. The man climbing on the rail stumbled and took a couple with him. The man on deck panicked and jumped over the side. The canoes sped away. I blew my hand whistle to summon the watch sailors. Nobody came. Then I realised that I was on my own. Thankfully the pirates didn't realise this, and did not come back. It was very comforting when we went alongside. Our neighbour and golf partner ran an exporting business, and had complained that a container had disappeared. He gave me the number, and sure enough, there it was, on the quay. Empty of course, but with 2 families installed.

Next to Takoradi to load more logs. Takoradi was a very important and big log port. Log rafts were floated to the ship and picked up straight from the water. Some of these were over 20 tons in weight. Nice photo of the ship alongside painted up ready for home. The swimming pool was now in full operation, and much appreciated.

Next to Abidjan. This is approached through a narrow entrance on the beach, which opens out into a very lovely lagoon, where you anchor, and load cargo from lighters. A modern French port. The French operate a very effective form of apartheid based on the cost of living.

Last loading port was Freetown, and then full speed to Tilbury. Time away, 11 weeks.

Automedon (Coasting)
September 1976

After 6 weeks' leave I was sent to Glasgow to join the *Automedon*. Same ship, same Chinese crew, big welcome. Work was quiet whilst some maintenance was completed. Dot, and some other wives duly joined us for the coasting around to the Continent. In the meantime, the bosun had decided to throw another party as a thank you to the officers. The sailors were soon to go back to Hong Kong. All were invited, and this took place on the night that most of them arrived. The food and hospitality were terrific, and we didn't have to worry about watchkeeping. What an introduction for the girls. As was traditional, we adjourned to the Officers bar just after 2100, and gin was served in pint pots. Not enough small glasses, and stores had not been replenished. We were on deep sea articles, so duty free prices applied.

After a few days, we sailed down the Irish Sea, around Lands End, and up the channel to Antwerp. The weather was fine and it was very pleasant. There was a smashing atmosphere on board. Cargo loading started, and some of the girls did some sightseeing. Dot fell in love with the 3rd Engineer, who was the double of Oz from Auf Wiedersein Pet. Sadly, so did the others. There's no accounting for taste.

Then to Rotterdam. Here we loaded direct from some of the very large barges. See the pictures. Most of us were able to go ashore, and the girls were duly impressed, shocked, amused, dismayed, when we accidentally walked down some of the streets where the local ladies were displaying themselves in their nighties, in their front rooms, for the benefit of passing trade.

Next, to Hamburg. The deepsea crew rejoined and took over, but there was time for one night ashore, which included a quick visit to 5 mark alley, another street of ill repute, before flying home. The girls had had their eyes opened to the benefits of joining the Common Market.

"We would like you to become involved with tankers. We think you would enjoy it," they said. They were right. Most seafarers were apprehensive of tankers, myself included, but I was persuaded and curious. You will need to attend a 5 day course in Southampton. This I duly did in December, and I found it to be very interesting. A totally new form of seafaring, and philosophy.

El Brega

14 December 1976-10 March 1977

"There's been a change of plans. We would like you to fly out to Singapore to join the El Brega. Afraid you will be away for Christmas." This was a big blow, but the company had been very good to me last year, and had relieved me so that I could be at home, so I had to go.

The Chief Officer will be on daywork, and you will be the Extra 2nd Officer, on the 12-4, and responsible for the navigation, a job that you are already doing. One major difference being that you had to do the worldwide chart corrections, a job normally done at the end of each voyage in the UK. Tankers could go to any pat of the world. The charts, hundreds of them, had to be kept up-to-date. This was done by reference to the Notice to Mariners which was issued weekly by the Admiralty, and involved very fine art and printing with special pens and ink. Unfortunately these Notices would arrive in batches at some ports. They were very time consuming.

The company had a manning arrangement for two Libyan tankers. This created some interesting situations. Brits manning a Libyan Government owned vessel, which was on charter to the Yanks. A previous voyage to an Israeli port had raised some tense moments for the authorities, and a subsequent visit to a homeport, Tripoli, had meant that Israeli egg boxes had had to be hidden.

You will fly from Heathrow to Kuala Lumpar; the ship is in Port Klang. Renamed from Port Swettenham, a place that I knew well from Blue Funnel days. The ship should have finished discharging, and will then go to Java to load for the Bahamas. Should be interesting.

The flight was overnight, a Boeing 747, a first time for me on this model, and very full. We seemed to have a fifth engine, suspended under the wings. Apparently this was a spare. Jumbos always look very slow and lumbering to me when they take off, but she managed OK. Stops were scheduled at Teheran and Bombay. There was nothing to see, rather boring, and I never sleep properly on a plane. Teheran came and went. A request to visit the cockpit was granted, and I spent a very pleasant time there. It was a quiet period in the flight, so we were able to compare our different navigation and safety systems, and I felt that they were happy to have someone to talk to. It must be difficult to keep alert when you are cooped up in a small space for a long time. At least on a ship's bridge you can wander around. The stop at Bombay took a bit longer due to refuelling, and a number of people left. Some more joined, but there was more space. I didn't leave the plane, but took the opportunity to have a good walk up and down. Those planes

Christmas carols,
Botantical Gardens

Flower clock

Orchid house

138

are huge. We landed at KL at 2200, where a taxi driver met me. There has been a change of plan. The ship has sailed to Java. You will stay the night here, and be flown to Singapore in the morning. It was quite a long drive, to not far from Port Klang. The hotel was very basic, very clinical, no reception, no en suite or refreshment facilities, and the bed was very hard. Even so, I dropped off immediately. Thankfully, I was not disturbed. Its time to go, its 0600, the shuttle is waiting. On reflection, I think the hotel was a licensed brothel, and I have no doubt that the driver was well rewarded, by his friends. By now it was a lovely hot tropical morning. There was the usual booking in time, so I had the opportunity to take photos of the famous airport clock and the plane. Each clock is set to a different cities time. Sadly most were wrong. Ah well. Nice thought. Unfortunately there was very limited refreshment facilities. I was hungry and tired. Duly boarded the Singapore Airlines shuttle. Very efficient and helpful, but no food. Just coffee. A good flight, but most of it was spent dodging the huge tropical thunderclouds. We had a safe landing at Changi airport, one of the most beautiful in the world, with flowerbeds and shrubs planted between the runways. Here, a very smart Chinese company office clerk met me. There has been a change of plan. We don't know where the ship is, so we will put you in the Marco Polo hotel. After my recent experience, I was a bit apprehensive. However, I was reassured that it was owned by the company, and was the third best hotel in Singapore. It was. It was lovely. A huge suite, with all facilities. Air conditioned, of course. Every night an orchid and piece of chocolate appeared on the pillow. Only problem, I had no money. Usually I travelled with just enough cash to get by, and had expected to be whisked straight to the ship. There was also a foreign currency limit. A 5 star hotel had not been considered. Next day I was taken to the office, where I was given some subsistence money. It wasn't very much, and I queried the amount. Later I was told that I was right, but in

Hotel pool

Marco Polo Hotel

Singapore boulevard

the meantime I had to get on with it. Singapore is a wonderful place, but very expensive. Not a place to be short of funds. I was introduced to a West African sailor from Freetown, who was also to join the same ship. It was his first time away from home, so I took him under my wing, but he didn't want to venture far, although I visited him regularly, and invited him out if I was going for a walk.

The hotel had a very nice swimming pool, which was quiet during the day. So I spent some time there. Occasionally an aircrew would stop over, but they kept themselves to themselves, and it was noticeable that flight and cabin crews tended to keep apart. Singapore is pretty flat, and the Botanical Gardens were not far away, so I had some nice walks. The world famous 'Orchid House' was well worth a visit, as shown in the photos. Orders were despatched to restaurants and hotels worldwide. On Sunday I was told that there would be a film shown at the Hilton Hotel nearby, on the roof top terrace. *The Battle of Britain*. It was a lovely tropical evening. There was a bar, swimming pool with screen at one end, and seating area at the other. The views over Singapore Island were breathtaking, with planes landing and taking off in the distance. The pool reflected the screen, so we had low flying Spitfires zooming in across the water. Who needs special effects. A couple of Tiger beers lasted a long time.

It was of course the build up to Christmas. The shops and the whole area were full of it. The Orientals are quite happy to take anybody's money, and are very enthusiastic. In the Botanical Gardens there is a lake, and arrangements were made for a children's carol concert one evening. It was a very lovely occasion, as the photos show. However the whole experience was not an easy time to be on your own, and away from the family. It was hard, and I was missing them. But I knew that they would cope and enjoy themselves.

Eventually the message came that the ship was on its way back, and that we would be collected at 2200. The stay had been for 10 days. We embarked onto a sampan and set off into the harbour. It was very dark, and you couldn't see much. After a while we came alongside this very large shape. We clambered up a rope ladder that had been suspended over the side of the foredeck. Being fully loaded, the deck was only 10 feet above the water. Here I was met and whisked off, via a lift, to the Officers mess. A big welcome, a beer, a snack, and I started to meet some of my new shipmates. A very friendly reception. The Chief Officer, Harry Hathaway, was the only one that I knew. Yes, he was the ringleader of the Sulima funnel job, and I had met him a few times since. We got on well. He was very professional, and knew his job thoroughly. He was in a class of his own. He had his wife with him. After a while I was shown to my cabin, where my luggage was waiting for me. However I had just been told that I was to do the anchor watch. Welcome back to reality. The bridge was huge, and a mass of incomprehensible dials and instruments. Being quiet I was able to start to familiarise myself, and some of the important ones had been pointed out to me. The company Agent had told the Captain about my bar bill of over £100, but had realised that they had not paid me the right subsistence. The matter would be reviewed. In fact, after the voyage was over, the Captain kindly wrote to me, to say that the Directors had decided to waive the matter. A big sigh of relief. We sailed in the evening, and made our way slowly up the Malacca Strait and into the Indian Ocean. Through the area affected by the recent Tsunami, of December 2004.

The ship was easily the biggest that I had ever been on. But a tiddler compared to some of the other supertankers around. Built in Japan in 1973, length 755 feet, breadth 125 feet, draft 49 feet, height of bridge 80 feet. Speed 15 knots. Fully loaded, 90,000 tons. To stop, 5 miles.

A totally different concept to seafaring. The atmosphere on board was tremendous. The ship was nearly always at sea. Ports were usually very remote, and in the middle of nowhere. Over the years a social life had developed. There would be a pub lunch on Sunday, and a pub dinner on Wednesday, so that all watchkeepers could share. Instead of formal meals with service, a couple of hot dishes and a buffet would be set out, dress would be casual smart, and informality would take over. Often an event would be organised, cards, films, bingo etc. Videos and films would be changed regularly. Crew changes were a major event. Newcomers made very welcome. Any tensions would be tackled. If the weather was reasonable, there would be a weekly cricket match on Sunday morning, between the deck and engineer departments, on the foredeck. Oil and water. This was serious stuff. Some of the West African crew would go to watch, from the walkway that ran down the foredeck, complete with cans of lager. Harry had told the opposition that I was a member of the MCC. This meant a hostile reception awaited me. Thanks Harry, but I did have the advantage of having played regularly. He was pretty useful himself, and we usually won. I would then go on my watch. Around 1300, when the pub lunch was in full flow, I would make a short sports news flash on the ship's tannoy, summarising the morning's events. Apparently this went down quite well with the deck mob, and the system had to be tested anyway. David Coleman has since retired.

We had a 3 week crossing of the Indian Ocean. A very pleasant, balmy, tropical time. A good opportunity to catch up with my chart corrections. We were due to call at Mauritius to take some diesel oil for the generators. Out of a six-week ocean passage, yes, you are right, it would be Christmas Day. As most of the crew would be involved, the festivities were deferred a day. As you can see, we anchored quite a way off, and an oil barge came out to us, together with some mail from home. Always welcome. Festive traditions were duly observed, very enjoyable, but we were still on watches, so it was not quite the same. We sailed south to the Cape of Good Hope, where you are

Atlantic spray

Helicopter crew change

actually quite close to the land, and could pick up the local radio stations clearly. Very homely, and you could see the fields and farmhouses. The countryside looked very abundant. A pleasant part of the passage.

We had to pass Capetown to change some of the crew and collect some stores using a helicopter. This involved slowing down to 12 knots and steering a course as advised by the pilot. There was a gentle swell and very balmy conditions. All round us seals sun bathing on the surface. Very often with one flipper up, and then they would swap round and expose the other. Capetown and Table Mountain were very clear, but distant. The chopper arrived, with a large cargo net suspended underneath. This was lowered to the deck and included stores, baggage, and crates of wine that we had been able to order beforehand. Very civilised. The crewmembers duly changed over, and we resumed our course. This time, north westerly.

We were on our own again and we didn't see any ships for days on end. Still had to keep alert. Routine continued, but gradually the weather changed, and sadly the cricket gear was swept overboard by seas. Depression engulfed the ship, but we were heading back into the northern hemisphere winter. Eventually we arrived off the Bahamas, but as we approached we picked up a SOS message. This we passed on to the Coastguard, and we could just see a helicopter in the distance rescuing a family, and their dog, from a yacht.

We were told that there was a queue in front of us for a few days. It is too deep to anchor there, but the conditions were such that you simply stopped engines and drifted. Another first for me. After a couple of days you simply steamed back to the top, and started drifting again. One had to keep within VHF range. There were about 20 huge leviathans doing this. Eventually we were called in, 0200 of course. My first docking on a big ship. Everything was done very slowly and methodically. The engines are ineffective above 5 knots. The slightest movement put huge stresses on the ropes. The mooring winches were special. The boarding Pilot and I had a big surprise, as we knew each other well from my insurance days. The discharge was very efficient. We were ordered to load 70,000 tons of oil for the power station at Sandwich, near Boston. Kennedy country. It was a severe winter and the Kennedy family were feeling the cold. Call in the cavalry. Us. The passage up was uneventful, but the weather deteriorated, and became a lot colder, in fact, very cold. We entered the Cape Cod Canal safely, and started to discharge. The radio stations gave us a big welcome. We were then told that we were the biggest ship to go there, that there was not enough space to turn us around off the dock, and that we would have to keep going through the canal when we left. Unfortunately, in some places there was not enough depth of water for us, and some of the bridges were too low for our masts and radar scanners. Get out of that one Brit. This led to huddles with the Captain, Chief Officer, Chief Engineer and the Pilot. The Mate, Harry, was the most experienced. When the ship was empty of cargo, the weight of the engine and accommodation meant that the stern was deeper than the bow. We could level the ship, but the masts would then be too high for the bridges. The ship's drawings, tide tables, tape measurements, draft readings, and whisky were consulted. Solution, the chief Officer would man the pump room, The two 2nd mates would be in their normal 'Stand by positions' at the bow and stern, The Chief Engineer would be down below. The first bridge was immediately after we left the berth, but there was depth of water available. We duly left, and cast off the tugs. Ballast water was pumped to deepen the stern, but we only expected clearance of a couple of feet. My station was aft, and we had a few anxious minutes as we went under. Any dislodging of parts, and we were in the bombing zone, with no shelter. There was of course a helicopter close by, complete with television crew, to catch the Brits deliberately smashing up there lovely and only bridge. Sorry to disappoint you Yank.

There was 5-foot clearance, which at 150 feet looked very close. As soon as we cleared, we had to transfer 20,000 tons of water to level the ship. The Chief Officer did this very quickly, and we passed the shallow water. The chopper had of course cleared off. How sad. The worst was over, or was it? What they did not tell us, was that Buzzards Bay, that we had to go through, was iced over, that some quite large ships were stranded, including tugs, and people were driving over the ice in places, and that we had to keep going. An empty tanker is not built to cope with ice. If we had stuck, we would have been crushed, and the ship lost. We would of course also have been booked for parking on double yellow lines on a main thoroughfare. The Pilot must have known this. Needless to say he did not get any more tea, or whisky. In fact he nearly had to ski home. We proceeded very gingerly. It was my bridge watch, so I could see what was happening. We were having to back and fill, i.e.: forward a bit, then astern a bit, to try and keep space around the hull, all the time trying not to damage the ships plates. In the later stages, when we were a mile from open water, we had less than 20 feet of water around us. Big ships have at least two levels of intakes for seawater for cooling the main engine. One low down for when the ship is light, and one nearer the waterline for using when loaded. We were having severe heating problems. The lower intake was sucking in mud and debris when we tried that, but the upper one was sucking in broken ice and debris when we used that. The Chief Engineer was on the controls by now, and there were frantic telephone discussions between bridge and engine room. Keep going or we are done for, no we cant, she's going to blow. Eventually we cleared the ice and set sail at full speed. Just about remembered to drop off the Pilot. Proceed to the open sea to clean 2 tanks, and await orders. There were some very severe messages between the Captain, Company, and Agent. The ship had been put at risk. Tank cleaning is also very dangerous, but passed off smoothly.

*New Orleans
Paddle Steamer*

*Kuala Lumpar
airport clock*

*Singapore
trishaw*

Go to South Riding Point in the Bahamas to load for St James on the Mississippi River. This was completed quickly, and we had a pleasant run off Cuba and Florida with many private cruisers and aeroplanes around. The U.S. Coastguard was also very active. On the lookout for drugs, immigrants and oil spillage. We entered the approaches in daylight. My first impressions being of a very wide river, a vast area of low muddy land. We had a pilot on board and kept up full speed, even going past New Orleans. On the way up you occasionally saw clumps of trees growing from the riverbank, with an old car stuck in the middle of the branches. They have parking problems here as well, or could it be the result of floods and hurricanes. Passing New Orleans was an experience, the radio stations, the music, the famous paddle steamers, but we were going 30 miles the other side, to the middle of nowhere. Vast, flat brown fields, hardly any housing or trees, but with riverbanks that had been built up, and a few tanker moorings added. The discharge didn't take long and we set off in the early hours. Once again at full speed. I am amazed that there have not been horrific accidents in the river.

Proceed to Pta Cardon in Venezuela to discharge some residual oil, and empty the slop tank, a smaller tank that was used to collect tank cleanings and surplus oil. The voyage was uneventful, and the weather became warmer. We passed the Cayman Islands and Jamaica in daylight. We tied up at the end of a very very long jetty; we could hardly see the shore. The Old Man and Mate dashed ashore to see if there was any visible damage to the bow. Thankfully, there was none. From there we were told to go to Freeport again for bunkers and a small crew change. We were then told to proceed into the middle of the Atlantic for orders. Here we were told to go to Malta for a major crew change. Details to follow. Spirits uplifted.

At dawn we stopped off Malta, a naval patrol boat came out with our reliefs, and we flew home. We only had time for a brief wander around Valetta. You could sense the spirit of history in every step. This voyage had been a terrific eye opening experience, and helped me considerably with my Master's ticket. Time away, 13 weeks.

There then followed some more coasting, so that I would be ready to start my Master's course at the end of April 1977.

I was on Duty, & on the BRIDGE for the "Cleveland Ledge Channel"

A HAZARDOUS PASSAGE FOR 'EL BREGA'

The following report of transit of Cape Cod Canal and ice conditions encountered in Buzzards Bay has been received from the Master of 'El Brega', Captain J. C. Ray:—

"Departure Sandwich was planned for 1030 hours 29th January – dead low water at the eastern end of the canal – and with up to minute information of tidal height readily available, departure draft and trim was re-adjusted to 27'00"F 29'00A to ensure maximum underkeel and overhead clearances for the first bridge 13 cables into the canal from our power station berth.

After discussion with the pilot Captain J. Lister and having seen the capabilities of the only 3 available tugs – max. HP 220 – during berthing I agreed with his opinion that they would be of no help during transit. They were, therefore, accordingly dismissed soon after clearing the berth.

Sagamore Bridge was cleared at 1104 hours with an estimated margin of 8 to 9 feet and the final lift railway bridge at Buzzards Bay at 1156 hours with the tide then at 2 hours flood giving an estimated overhead clearance of 3 to 4 feet. A continuous echo-sounder trace indicated a depth in excess of the

minimum 32 ft. MLW declared by the authorities. However, Captain Lister assured me such spots do exist but being solid rock cannot be reduced without blasting and risk of damage to the canal banks and adjacent properties.

Having successfully cleared the Canal Land Cut it was disturbing but initially not alarming to meet increasing quantities of brash ice in Hog Island Channel. However, at 1250 hours in Cleveland Ledge Channel, we entered a field of solid packed and rafted ice, estimated thickness one foot. We had no option but to attempt to force passage to known clear water almost 7 miles ahead. This took in all 3 hours 37 minutes, including two stops totalling 1 hour 23 minutes to allow the main and auxiliary machinery to cool down before continuing passage. During this period which I would commend to you sterling efforts of Chief Engineer Mr S Cooper and his staff who, in most extreme and difficult conditions and

circumstances, prevented the ever-present likelihood of a "black out" and its attendant dangers.

Captain Lister was equally unaware of the conditions we were to encounter before we left our berth in Sandwich and if this information had been available to me I would have remained alongside until conditions improved. It was noticeable that within an hour of passing US Coastguard Cod Canal Station a Notice to Mariners was issued closing the canal to all shipping until further notice due to the ice conditions in Buzzards Bay.

I would also take this opportunity to commend to you the interest shown and the care and attention taken by Chief Officer Mr H Hathway and all the other officers in confirming measurements, draft readings etc. during preparation for the transit which created a "record" in the canal's history. 'El Brega' is now the largest ship to pass through in terms of deadweight, beam and overall height.

Christmas Day at Mauritius

Mauritious at anchor.

Masters

April - December 1977

Arrangements had been made for me to stay with my cousin Erica and her husband Mark, who owned a big house in the Everton district of Liverpool, within walking distance of the Polytechnic. I would travel up on Sunday afternoon, and return home on Friday evening. I was easily the oldest on the course, but was made very welcome and given a lot of help by the others, in fact we worked well as a group. The course would be for 6 months, and involved 6 written papers, as well as an 'oral' exam. After a while I developed a routine of stopping at 10 pm, but starting revision and study at 7 am. This seemed to work.

There wasn't much time for socialising, but one of the tutors was a keen cricketer, and organised a departmental team. This involved a weekly evening 20 over match, and we developed a strong team. Very enjoyable, and I did well. Later he arranged a 'staff v student' game on a Sunday afternoon at the 'Odyssey' ground in Aigburth. It was a lovely day, with wives and families present. Peter guested for us. I was captain, we won, and we all had our moments. I think some of the staff were rather pleased, as they usually won, and their leader was not the most popular in the staff room. There was a very good celebration later.

Occasionally Mark and I would go for a pint. He is a very keen cricket enthusiast, so we had plenty to talk about. As a solicitor, he did a lot of prosecutions. Guys would come up to him, "How are you Mark?", have a pint and after they had wandered off, he would tell me that he had had them put down not long ago. They accepted this, and he got on very well with them. An incredible man. Now a High Court Judge, involved with some very high profile cases.

151

CERTIFICATE OF COMPETENCY

AS

MASTER

OF A FOREIGN-GOING SHIP   No.121087

To ——— Eden Stuart Mathews ———

WHEREAS you have been found duly qualified to fulfil the duties of Master of a Foreign-going Ship in the Merchant Navy, the Board of Trade in exercise of their powers under the Merchant Shipping Acts and of all other powers enabling them in that behalf hereby grant you this Certificate of Competency.

Dated this 13th day of September 1978

Countersigned

Registrar General.   An Under Secretary of the Board of Trade

REGISTERED AT THE OFFICE OF THE REGISTRAR GENERAL OF SHIPPING AND SEAMEN

Signature of the person to whom this Certificate is issued

Year of Birth: NINETEEN HUNDRED AND THIRTY-SEVEN
Place of Birth: WEYMOUTH, DORSET
This Certificate is given upon an Examination passed on the 3rd day of JULY 1978
Issued at the Port of CARDIFF
on the 20th day of SEPTEMBER 1978
P.J.Q. ..... Supt.
Radar Simulator Course Attendance Certificate No. L 2446
dated the 1st day of OCTOBER 1976

If any person forges or fraudulently alters, or assists in forging or fraudulently altering, or procures to be forged or fraudulently altered any Certificate of Competency, or an Official Copy of any such Certificate, or makes, assists in making, or procures to be made, any false Representation for the Purpose of procuring either for himself or for any other person a Certificate of Competency; or fraudulently uses a Certificate or Copy of a Certificate of Competency which has been forged, altered, cancelled or suspended, or to which he is not entitled; or fraudulently lends his Certificate of Competency or allows it to be used by any other person, that person shall in respect of each offence be guilty of a Misdemeanour.—Section 104 of the Merchant Shipping Act, 1894.

NOTE.—Any person finding this Certificate must send it to the Registrar General of Shipping and Seamen, Cardiff, CF5 2YS, postage unpaid.

O-433/007 DD.545758 400 5/75 (R&T Nasten.)

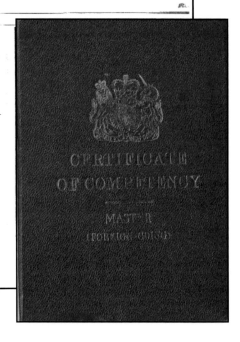

It was recommended that we should take our 'Orals' before the writtens. One less thing to worry about. Most of us agreed, and this lead to frantic revision and study. Mostly in small groups, but it paid off, as we all passed. The 'Oral' exam was a chilling experience. The examiner could ask about anything and everything, and could make the occasion very difficult. I seemed to start all right, and when he established my Conway and Blue Funnel training, things seemed to go smoothly. Possibly knowing what I was talking about had helped. Huge sense of relief.

The 'Written's' were at the end of November. 5 exams of 2 hours, with a minimum pass mark on each, and an overall average pass of over 70%. Any failure, and the rest of the papers were not marked. Nor were you told where you had failed, but usually you knew. I did. One question in Magnetism did me. So, back to the drawing board. Not everybody passed.

During the summer, I had become aware of the Geest Line. Regular 23 day trips from Barry to the West Indies seemed very attractive. However, I was now out of leave and needed to top up cash and reassess the situation. There were discussions with my employers and the college. Some more coasting followed. However, there was a short revision course starting in May. In January I found myself in Avonmouth with a bit of time on my hand so I travelled to Geest for an interview which was successful, and I joined in mid-February as 2nd mate. This took me up to join the course. Some very intense swotting, but this time I was successful. Yippee, not bad for an old man.

Passenger Information ⌇ **The Geest Line**

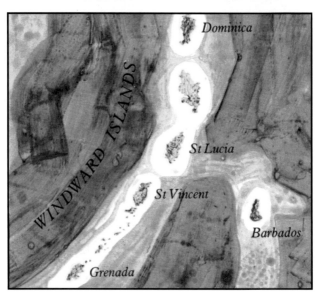

Geest Line

February 1978 - January 1980

The company was fairly new, founded in 1952 by the Dutch family Geest. They had developed a very high quality banana trade to the Windward Islands. In fact they dominated the commercial trade. However, they were a very responsible company, and had helped to give the islands significant independence. They operated 4 modern and fast specialist refrigeration ships, with weekly sailings from Barry. They carried 12 first class passengers.

Outward they would carry up to 1,500 tons of general cargo, including fertiliser and hundreds of used car tyres. On one occasion we carried a very expensive luxury motor cruiser. Homeward it would be 2,000 tons of bananas in 152,000 boxes, and over 100 tons of exotica, mangoes, limes, grapefruit, coconuts etc. in chilled lockers. The bananas covered the running costs of the voyage, whilst the outward cargo and passengers provided the profit. Hopefully.

The ships were 490 feet long, 5,900 tonnes, sea speed 21 knots. (Almost 25 m.p.h.). Because the priority was for speed, they did not have the usual bilge keels to reduce the rolling. This could be very heavy at times, up to 35° each way. Good fun, but sometimes frightening.

A typical voyage would start with sailing on Thursday afternoon, through the lock, and out into the Bristol Channel. Drop the Pilot, and soon you were past Lundy Island and out of sight of land. After a few days of sailing into the Atlantic, often with very mixed weather, conditions would usually improve after passing the Azores. On my first voyage in January, on the *Geestland*, we went straight into a force 10 storm, becoming 12, and were 3 days late to Barbados. At one time, when we were in the trough of the waves, we could not see over the top of the waves. The bridge was 60 feet above the water. Some Captains liked to go through the Islands, others to keep well away.

Once the sea conditions settled, a highlight of the voyage would be the Barbecue. This would be instead of dinner, and on the outside passenger deck. All officers and passengers would be invited, but watchkeepers would have to be sensible. A large empty oil drum would be set up, filled with charcoal, and trellis tables arranged. High quality steaks, drumsticks, sausages etc followed, dutifully washed down by the appropriate liquid. Usually very happy occasions and the *Geestland* had its own very good Steel Band. As Chief Officer on the 4-8, I would join late, and had to make up for lost time. On one instance I arrived to see the Senior Captain wiping his pristine white uniform trousers to remove the contents of a full plate of goodies. Thanks Dot. End of all promotion hopes, but David Boon and I remained good friends. David and I had met at a Shrewsbury Golf Club dinner, where he had been very enthusiastic about Geest, and was one of the reasons why I became interested in the company.

Barbados would be the first port of call to start discharging. Normally you would arrive at 0500 to dock ready to start cargo at 0700. Sometimes you would load a small amount of inter island cargo. Passengers and off duty crew would then enjoy the island. On one occasion the Kerry Packer cricket circus was in town. West Indies against Australia. Most of the big names playing. I made enquiries with the stevedores as to the chance of getting in. The ground was walkable from the dock. Go to gate 3 and ask for security man Fred. He will see what he can do. Contact was duly established, and I was hustled into a very dark grandstand. It was very full. Play had started. When my eyes became accustomed to the light, I realised that I was the only white man there. There had been some tensions recently. Very quickly I became an avid Windies supporter. When my neighbours realised that I was just another enthusiastic cricket fan, and anti-Aussie, I was quietly accepted, in fact a can of Heinekens, unopened, was thrust into my hand. Lovely people. Sadly I had to leave at 1730, to rejoin the ship for dinner and then sailing. Departure was usually at, or after dinner. This routine applied to the outward ports of Castries in St Lucia, Kingstown in St Vincent, and finally St George's in Grenada. Possibly the loveliest early morning arrival that I have experienced anywhere in the world. The harbour is a small horseshoe. On the left as you approach is a spur of land with a low hill. On top is built a large imposing stone police station. As you follow round you will see houses, some brick or stone, some wooden, all painted in different bright colours, and interspersed with bougainvillea and other exotic plants. The sun would rise slowly over the police station, and the rays would pick out the different colours. The promenade ran around the bay, only 2 feet above the waters edge, to the dock area. This was parallel to the shore, and big enough for two ships. We were priority, and berthed at the town end. There was hardly any tide. It was also the end where the boats from the cruise ships anchored outside, would land their passengers, to be greeted by a steel band. All very jolly. It was also the end where the very very fast drug smuggler speed canoes from Venezuela assembled.

Grenada is known as the Spice Island, and a visit to the stalls in town was always very interesting. It also has a very lovely beach, Gran Danse. The beach is gently curving, about a mile long, with soft sand about 20 yards wide running into palm groves. Some small luxury bungalows have been discreetly built, with plenty of space between them. Peter Ustinov used to hire one when he wanted privacy to learn a new film script. On the voyage that Dot did, one of the passengers, a wealthy raspberry farmer from Scotland, who had his daughter with him, hired one and invited some of us to join him. We had a lovely day, and it was there that we met Les Dawson. I recognised him

as he came out of the sea, we called him over, and he just started chatting very naturally. The humour flowed. After a few minutes he excused himself to go and join another group nearby, which was his first wife and family. I think she died a couple of years later. They were on the cruise ship Cunard *Countess* that called in regularly, and we usually had to move our ship along to let her on to the quay. That was one of my jobs.

Grenada was the only stop where we had a scheduled overnight stay. The first day would be to finish discharging, sweeping the hatches and making preparations for the bananas. This would start at 0700 and continue throughout the day. On one occasion when I was on early duty, I ambled out as usual, before time, to check that everything was ready, when I was called over to the Islands Cargo Officer, a West Indian, who always joined each ship to liaise with the stevedores. It was a beautiful day. Listen to this he said. He had his portable radio tuned in to the BBC World Service. *'There are reports of an armed coup on the island of Grenada!'* We immediately switched to the local radio. Martial music, heavy martial music. This went on for sometime and I alerted the Captain. After a while there was an announcement. *'Dis am de glorious freedom fighters, we have come to save you from de wicked President. Do not be alarmed. We are visiting all the Police and Fire Stations. If you support us, please put a white flag on a pole. If not, we will call to persuade you. Already we have the support of....'.* This was followed by more martial music. This must be a standard insurgent script and procedure, as I had heard it before in Nigeria. This was a communist plot led by Maurice Bishop. The stevedores were understandably slow to arrive, but cargo did start. We were in a funny position. A British ship, with white officers in the middle of an armed political coup. What a lovely hostage, or target. Anyway, a Russian cruise liner tied up ahead of us, with its stern tied to the wharf and bow anchored at right angles into the harbour. There was also another cruise liner at anchor outside.

Grand Dans Beach

La Toc pool

Les Dawson

Both ships duly despatched their tourist boats to the landing stage near us. Steel band in full flow. Around mid morning two taxis suddenly appeared and raced to the fire Station near the dock entrance. Bodies hanging out of the windows, all brandishing guns, with a big flag flying from a very long aerial. This was the fighting force. There was a pause. Tourists gathered with their cine cameras whirring away, a flag appeared, loud cheers, taxis departed, crowd dispersed. Cargo restarted. Then something started to stir near the big Police Station. The radio confirmed that all the Fire and Police stations had been accounted for. We then saw men clambering up the bank towards the building with their guns. Shots were exchanged. A policeman's arm appeared with revolver, more shots, it was withdrawn, and then appeared in the next window. More shots. Withdrawn. Men clambering over the balustrades. More shots from inside. Then silence. What was going on? This was the headquarters of an unpopular regime, and this was where all the security files were kept. Eventually the radio told us that the victory was complete. The supply of bananas started to peter out, and the decision was taken to sail forthwith. Traditionally this is the time when all good and successful freedom fighters celebrate a good day's work with the local hooch. And what could be more fun than taking a pot shot at a wicked white colonialist in full view, only 50 yards away. My station was on the poop, the closest point to the best bar. A decision that I fully endorsed, and I risked reprimand by not changing into my white uniform as normal, dirty khakis being less conspicuous. There was no comment. Safe departure, much to the relief of the Captain and everybody on board, including the cargo officer. We were later told that a dozen men had taken control of the garrison where two novices had been on sentry duty. They had been overcome, there were two deaths, and the armoury requisitioned. Recent political propaganda says that there were 'no deaths'. I don't think so! The Americans became alarmed when the new leaders started to

*St. Vincent
farmer*

St Vincent market

St. Vincent harbour

Banana plantations

talk of a new runway big enough for the biggest jets, including bombers, and a missile site on top of the hills, well within range of the Mississippi oilfields and Florida. That is why they later invaded. Gran Danse beach being the landing zone, where the Holiday Inn awaited them. The Yanks know how to go to war. I could never understand why Maggie got so upset. The Yanks complained that the charts were 90 years old. We used the same charts, but we kept ours up-to-date. That was one of my jobs. Hills and cliffs, and beaches don't move all that much. Later satellite positioning showed that some of these positions were as much as 30 feet adrift. Not bad for rowing boat and sextant technology. Fair enough that, depths, buoyage, lights, buildings, foliage does change.

Overnight sail to St Vincent, dawn docking, and 0700 start loading. When Dot was with me, the Island vet and his wife kindly invited us for a drive around. They took us up into hills, past numerous small banana plantations Very twisty, very bumpy, very sweaty, but very interesting. We also visited Young Island, a very exclusive hotel on a small island, which has been featured in films. On another occasion, I was on cargo duty during the afternoon. The ship started to move around. There was no wind, no tide. Very eery. This gradually got worse. There had been some volcanic rumblings in Mt Soufriere. About 1700, the Captain and shore manager decided to stop cargo and secure the ship. The crew then went onto full stand by positions for departure. I was on the foc's'le, my normal position that voyage. I was still in my dirty cargo gear, and did not have time for a wash. We were issued with axes in case we had to cut the ropes, and wires. There we stayed, until I was given a 2 hour break for some sleep at 0600. Cups of tea and sandwiches occasionally appeared. The swell worsened, the ship was thumping into the wharf very heavily, and at 0400, the gangway was lowered and the passengers disembarked. I could see this quite clearly and thought that it was a very dangerous decision.

Despite the moorings, the ship was surging up to ten feet off the quay, and then slamming against it and heeling over. Some damage was done to the hull. Eventually we were able to sail later in the morning. Full speed. We put this down to pressure waves caused by the seismic activity, now called 'tsunamis'. The volcano did create problems for a while afterwards.

Usually we would depart about 1700 so that we could arrive at Vieuxfort in St Lucia ready for a 2200 start. This was at the request of the local women stevedores. It was too hot during the day. It did mean that the Chief Officer was lucky to get 2 hours broken sleep in 48. This was different. The ship's side doors are opened, and wide boards placed and secured up to the openings. They were quite steep. The women would carry 2, sometimes 3, banana boxes on their heads up to the waiting men. They would be given a tally for each box, and then run back down to collect more boxes. Hence Harry Belafonte's popular song, 'Hey Mr Talisman'. The men would be in chain line, and throw the boxes along it. They were very fast, and the stow was very accurate and tight. It was almost impossible to cross through from one side to the other if one needed to do. Part of our duties was to check the stowage, and keep an eye on the state of the fruit. Occasionally a box would be dropped, usually because the chuckers were faster than the stackers. The atmosphere was very intense but good-humoured. Finish about 0400, and immediately sail round the corner to Castries, dock at 0600, ready to start a day's work at 0700.

The pace would slacken off a bit now. Most decisions had been made, and it was just a question of filling up the ship. The banana berth was separate from the main docks, and was within walking distance to 'Bagshaws', the renowned Sea Island cotton shop. This was always worth a visit, and was also a short cut to the beach and the excellent 'La Toc' hotel. Superb swimming pool complex, and next to the beach. It was a short stroll into the sea. There was also a 9-hole golf course behind.

This could be very hot, and one had to be aware of the 'Fleur de Lis' adders, the only poisonous, and very dangerous, snake in the islands. They were introduced by the French to discourage escaping convicts and slaves. I never saw one.

The luxury cabin cruiser that I mentioned earlier had been discharged here. The Captain and I had of course opened it up, to inspect and check the interior. We were under strict instructions to treat it with kid gloves. The owner turned up to observe. The Bosun took the controls of the crane, and I took charge on deck. There was very little room around the boat, and the slightest swing or sway would have caused damage, and all sorts of unhappiness. We worked well together, and the lift was flawless. The boat was lowered into the water with no problems. The owner climbed down, inspected everything, started the motors, and came back on deck. He was thrilled. He was in his late 50s, had sold up everything at home, and was going to cruise around. He duly signed the various documents, bade farewell, and returned to his new toy. Ropes let go, a big wave of the arm as he looked up at the ship's onlookers, full speed ahead with both very powerful engines. Unfortunately the tiller was turned towards the ship. He scraped all the way along our newly painted hull, and damaged his boat. Much merriment on board. We did discuss sending him a bill. Departure in the evening, by this time everybody would be getting tired. Some more than others, even the passengers would find that a new port, a new island, new ventures everyday becomes a bit demanding. To Dominica was the longest inter island passage, and we sailed up past Martinique. Usually it was well lit up.

Dawn arrival. Dominica rises steeply out of the sea into a luxuriant green mountain. There is very little foreshore for anchoring, but just enough. It is the least developed of the islands. During the first few visits, we did anchor, and the bananas would be loaded from barges through the side doors. It was just a matter of filling up any spare spaces. However,

Discharging bananas in Barry

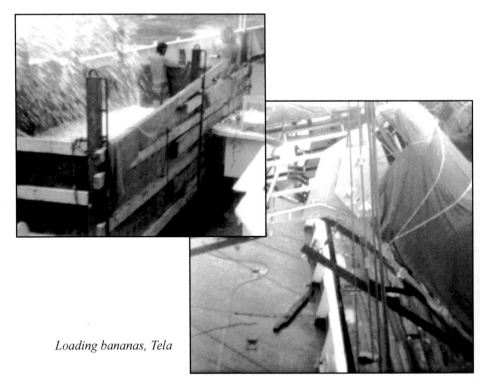

Loading bananas, Tela

a hurricane proof jetty was being built in the main seaport of Roseau. Strong steel girders, and designed to withstand winds of 120 m.p.h. It was well designed. Unfortunately a hurricane did hit full on. The island was devastated, including the new jetty. Mangled and twisted. Man cannot outdo nature. The island manager told us later of his 'beatle' car being lifted off the ground with his family in it. Thankfully he was able to hold on to it and nobody was hurt. The passengers usually enjoyed their last trip ashore, and would go up the mountain, mountain chicken being a delicacy. This would amuse us, as it was in fact a very large rat. Evening departure, and full speed to Barry.

The sea and weather would still be gorgeous, but it was time to catch up on rest, clean ship, paint ship, start repair lists etc. On the Tuesday, about 1000, you could usually see Concorde flying to Europe from Rio de Janeiro. Very high in the sky, but they used different wavelengths, so we could not speak to them. They would be home in a few hours, we had a week to go. The weather would start to deteriorate about the Azores, and of course sometimes could be very rough. There was of course the Fastnet yacht disaster, and there was the occasion when the German ship 'Munchen' disappeared without any signals. We were actually approaching the search zone, and being allocated an area, when it was called off. This event caused a lot of concern in seafaring circles, as she was a very new, large, modern, purpose built vessel. There was hardly any debris.

The bananas would be very closely monitored, air temperature as well as the fruit itself, and instructions from Barry would ensure that it was perfect for discharge. Speed would be adjusted for arrival on Sunday morning tide, usually 0400. The entrance to Barry dock is very tricky. The refrigerated vans would be waiting, The Marks and Spencer top grade would be first off to the ripening sheds, a chemical spray, and on to the shelves on Monday. Mail, crew instructions, management, repair meetings, safety inspection arrangements, handover to reliefs etc. This was a busy time. Usually we did two voyages on and one off, with just a short break in the middle, but as I was a relief Chief Officer, it didn't always work out like that.

As mentioned earlier, Dot was able to do a full round voyage. This was terrific, and she joined in happily. The 3 girls all came down for short visits at different times. One of these was an August evening in Barry, where the Steel Band had been persuaded to play for us, it was a lovely night, and the band was superb. They were good, and often played at Night Clubs in Cardiff.

This was a very enjoyable but hard going experience. Because of my age I felt that I was unlikely to be top of the list for promotion when younger, company experienced Mates would be available, so, as conditions were improving ashore, I started to look around, and wrote to BUPA to see if there would be a position in Shropshire. Private Health insurance was the in vogue flavour. There soon was, and it was good to be back with the family. As it was, a couple of years later, Geest sold out the banana trade to Elders & Fyffes, and the ships went on 6 monthly voyages from USA across the Pacific to Japan. This was brought about by the new EU requirements for straight bananas, and virtually bankrupted the islands. No thanks.

PART THREE

Childhood

Age 0-14

My Grandparents at my Christening

Fraser Allen and us on the farm

Mombasa Cathedral

170

IN THE BEGINNING

1937-1939

It all began on the 15th of April in 1937, a day of great joy and anticipation for the family. I have no recollection of the event. I was born in a small cottage in Weymouth in Dorset. Sadly I have never been back.

My mother was staying with her family for the birth, as my father was working in East Africa, an arrangement that was often made in those days. It did however mean, that I was the only member of my immediate family that was entitled to a full British passport, a situation that was to create a few problems in later years, when the immigration rules changed and the family wanted to return home. My father was born in Johannesburg South Africa, my mother in Uganda, and my sister in Kenya. Such was the legacy of the roving colonial and missionary families.

My father, Stuart, was a Manager for the agricultural firm Dalgetty's, in East Africa. He would do two year tours, which included local leave, and then had six months at home. His job was to supply stores and equipment to the farmers, and also to inspect and purchase their produce. This would often involve going up country on a safari to visit the outlying farms. The original man from Delmonte, or should it be Dalgetty. There were no motorways or permanent roads. The rains would wash them away. A journey could involve travelling overnight. No Travel Lodges, so he would simply park up in the bush, and sleep in his car. What about lions I would ask. He reckoned that a shot to the eyes would discourage further aggression. He always took his shotgun, was a very good shot, and was very confident. I can remember going with him on some of the closer visits, and on one occasion he condemned a pile of oranges, which was not very popular. Even I, as a young kid, could see that they were overripe. However, he did make a lot of friends, and we would sometimes go to stay on the farms. One such was Fraser Allen, who had a farm in the Rift Valley overlooking Lake Naivasha. This was usually covered with flamingos. Beautiful. Being up a hill, the weather was perfect. Cool overnight, with dew in the mornings, and hot during the day. The adults did a lot of fishing and shooting, in between farm duties. On one occasion we went to the local hamlet where a doctor was conducting a regular surgery for the locals. Most settlers took their responsibilities seriously, but of course there was no NHS, and the treatment was very basic, and the funds were limited. We played happily with the son David. Wildlife everywhere. Sadly Fraser was killed in a tractor accident. They lived in a large bungalow with nice lawns and garden surrounds. Natural flora and fauna. The guests stayed in a chalet which was corrugated iron with a lining of bamboo inside. All sorts of rustling at night. Very disturbing, but comfortable. His widow later married the farmer next door. Very convenient.

Where is Eden? I had disappeared. We had gone to another farm as guests. There's loud purring from the outhouse. The door was opened very gingerly. In the stable area was a Cheetah mother lying down with her young cubs, and I was playing happily with them. Extrication was very gentle. Apparently she had been injured and rescued from the bush, and was being nursed until after the birth, so that she could be returned to the wild. I was about four.

Dad was born in Johannesburg, but his parents died fairly young. He was brought up by his grandparents in Appleby in Cumberland, by the River Eden, which he later named me after. This is where he developed his great love of fishing. He was educated at St Bees together with his younger brother Robin. He was very good at sport being county class at badminton, and a very keen cricketer. From there he joined Barclays bank and rose to assistant manager, but he didn't enjoy this, although he was able to develop his love of cricket, and at one stage was credited with the fastest century on a county ground in a league match, at Penrith. He left the bank to join Dalgetty in East Africa. He was stationed at Mombasa and was a member of the Cathedral choir.

My mother was born in Uganda. Her father was a missionary with the C.M.S but her Mother died when she was very young. He later remarried, Annie Harvey, and they had three children. Rosemary, John and Eric. In due course they all went to St Michaels C.M.S School in Limpsfield, Surrey. This was a boarding school for missionary children, and was set in delightful surroundings, and they all had very fond memories. The school was very much a home from home, but with very good scholastic levels. My mother rejoined her family in Mombasa where her father was now Suffragen Bishop. I think that they were married in Nairobi Cathedral, but it was a few years before I was born.

Rosemary, I cannot remember and know very little about, although she was my godmother. She later married Tim Goldsmith the famous Australian Battle of Britain pilot ace. I met him briefly later in Sydney. Sadly she was lost at sea, when the troopship she was on was torpedoed, by the Japs, when she was travelling to join him in Australia. Tim was stationed in Cornwall, and was a regular visitor to the vicarage at Tuckingmill. He flew Hurricanes, and regularly would do a victory roll on his way back from training or sorties. He would be back for tea. He was stationed in Malta during their difficulties. Later, when Australia was threatened by Japan, he was transferred and based in Darwin. He flew many sorties, was shot down a few times, but eventually he was so badly injured, that he spent a long time in hospital. He married one of the nurses.

Eric joined the Army with the Duke of Cornwall Light Infantry, which he thoroughly enjoyed. It was his recommendation that resulted in my going to Beaumont House School, for which I am eternally grateful. Apparently he had done a relief job there in 1941, and was very impressed with the set up. Later during the war, he was seconded to the Kings African Rifles, and we saw him in Tanga, when he was recovering from malaria.

John joined the Colonial Service and became a District Commissioner in the Kano region of Northern Nigeria. He was also my Godfather, and we used to correspond regularly, every four years, even when I was at boarding school and first at sea. Such was the lines of communication then, but we always seemed close. He always made a point of visiting me at school, a wonderful man. He loved cricket, was a very useful medium/ fast bowler, and I was able to get him some games in Tunbridge Wells a few years later. Surely his claim to fame had to be to marry, in his early thirties, and produce two sets of twins within two years.

MY TIME IN KENYA & TANGA

1939-1944

With apologies to Lionel and Jean, but, I was there.

My mother and I travelled out on the British India ship *Mantola* in 1939, and joined my Father in Nairobi. He had arranged to build a house in Karan, an area a few miles from the city, which we duly moved into. At some stage Pam was born, but I was too young to recall these events.

I can remember a very flat rather barren area in the bush, with this fairly large thatched roofed house. There was a thatched summer house in the gardens. Most of my memories have been jogged by photographs. Sadly the house caught fire and was destroyed. Apparently I was running in and out trying to help rescue things, just what you would expect from a two year old. But my Teddy was saved, badly singed, and we travelled many miles and years happily together. Apparently the area was known for puff adders, which are a very nasty snake, but I do not remember seeing one. We had a beautiful Golden Retriever, Midas. He was an excellent gundog, and companion. This was the only house that my parents ever tried to buy. We were then transferred to Tanga. This involved hiring a covered rail wagon, which, after loading, was added to the back of a regular train. An area was created for the overnight journey. Camp beds, mosquito nets, chairs, paraffin stove, and a large jug of water. The rest of our furniture was in the other half of the space. There were a few other families also involved. There was quite a spirit of adventure.

Tanga was a small port on the banks of the Tana River near

Me in Karan garden

The house at Karan

Dad, Pam and me

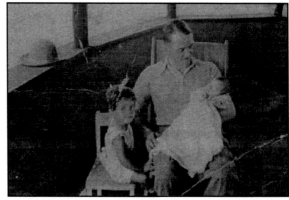

its mouth. My early memories are of a very flat area, a broad river with many small islands and a wreck in the middle. This was in fact a German freighter that had been sunk during the First War, and was a popular boat trip for locals and visitors. She was listing quite heavily, very rusty, and all her wooden decks had disappeared, thus exposing her deck beams.

There was a small new dock area for coasters and a jetty that was built on pillars with some steps leading into the water. I was told not to go down these, but of course spent many happy hours fishing from them. My speciality was a small silver fish with a yellow and black spot on its side. Inedible of course, but the cook (mpechi) did kindly try to cook one for me once, and we duly agreed with his assessment. Why a passing croc didn't take me for din dins I don't know, maybe they are choosey. On one occasion I did hook a sea snake in the dock basin, but dad took the line off me very quickly and cut the line. It was a horrible shivering experience. This didn't stop me fishing off the steps though.

We lived in an upstairs flat, in some buildings at the inland end of a very large compound, which was surrounded by high walls for security. Often there would be lorries and produce parked there, including piles of bales of sisal, very exciting, and we had no fear of what might be crawling in them.

There was another family in a near apartment, the Williams's. The father was very ill with T.B., and we didn't see much of him. He died later. The mother was pleasant, but very careworn. No state benefits then. They had a son who was older than us, and a daughter of my age that played with us.

The offices were at the other end of the compound, on the main road near to the river, but we didn't go there very often, although a Kindergarten school did open at the back later.

The flat consisted of four bedrooms, dining room, large lounge, kitchen and bathroom in a line, with a passage connecting them. Access was via an outside stone staircase which ran down the side of the building from a small balcony. The rooms were airy with large ceiling fans. Each bed had its own mosquito net suspended from the ceiling.

Alongside the building ran a busy street, with a monsoon ditch on each side, and opposite us were buildings with flats and shops, which seemed to house many Indian families. They were very noisy but colourful. However they did do us a big favour during a black out period, when we had covered our lights with papier-machee covers. These had protected whisky bottles during transit, and one of these had caught fire.

Nearby, on this road, was a garden area with a soft drink stall. We would sometimes be taken there as a family treat in the evening about sunset, and I could enjoy my "dragon's blood". Later in life I identified this as raspberryade. Pam had other tastes. Sunset was six'ish, and twilight lasted for half an hour, still very warm, but very pleasant. Happy memories.

From time to time there would be processions down the street, masses of people, very colourful, very noisy, often with statues or shrines carried on platforms on people's shoulders. Weddings, funerals, religious, there were many Hindus and Moslems in the area.

Donkeys, the market was half a mile away, they did a lot of baying and made a lot of noise, not the best of dawn chorus's. There was a little shop that specialised in coconut products, they did a very nice macaroon that I was partial to.

There was a gang of us, and we went all over the place. Somebody said that there was a python in the ruins of an old house nearby, so we had to go and investigate, well what else would any self-respecting six year old do. Despite a lot of prodding and poking we didn't find anything.

There's an octopus on the rocks near the dock, so off we trooped, but someone had got their first. The river was tidal and had a sandy beach, we loved that beach, and there was supposed to be areas of quicksand, but these didn't bother us. On one occasion we wandered upstream quite a long way and came across an area with a lot of cattle bones on, which we found to be very interesting, until chased away by the Governor's butler. We were close to the abattoir, and also the Governor's Residence. Sadly the Governor's eighteen year old daughter was knocked down and killed by a military lorry, in the blackout.

Keep off the streets, keep away from windows, there is a war exercise tomorrow. So we did, but we did have a peep. Soldiers, guns, casualties, stretcher parties, and shooting. Eventually the action moved further away, and the gang decided to venture out. We went on to the river road for a change, away from the activity, and were minding our business, when a military lorry drove by with a number of soldiers on, as they went we heard the ping of a bullet, this did not amuse us and we told them so, but by this time they were a long way off. So we went to look for the bullet, without success. Lousy shot, or was it a warning.

The Fleet Air Arm had a unit in Tanga. The local community decided to adopt them and entertained as best they could. This often involved drinks at home and Pam and I thoroughly approved. We were always spoilt, after all the lads were away from home and families, and we did well out of drinks and nuts, and occasional toys. I can remember being given a wooden model of a Gloucester Gladiator aircraft, which I cherished for many years. For a special treat I was taken out on a tugboat to witness, with others, the disposal of outdated flares and pyrotechnic signals on the river. Very exciting, a great day out. Although I do recall that there was some concern if they didn't ignite or go off.

Tanga had a very definite social strata. There were probably a few hundred families there, so people knew most of them, but not all. The bank manager was very important and whilst friendly and polite, kept his distance. Mr Swan, a shortish tubby man who wore baggy white shorts, as did the Padre. Sunday and church were very important, and most people attended. I recall an open sided building, and you could look out on to open

Aunt Molly and I

Escape!

Budding author

spaces. There were large fans in the ceiling which stirred the air, but it was still very hot, particularly during the day. Hard seats of course, but also loose cushions. The services seemed a bit long, but of course they would to a youngster, but I always felt at home. There's going to be a party. Goodie. Somebody's birthday. How nice. Outdoors. Of course. You will all dress up. Oh no. You are going to be a goblin. Oh hell. You will be in a green outfit with a fur hat. Oh mercy. Just what sort of way is this to treat a five year old. What sort of image in the gang. I fought, I resisted, I lost, and I hated it. I have never enjoyed dressing up since.

Dad loved cricket, and so did we. There was a ground just outside the town and he played regularly. He was a very good left handed positive batsman, and occasional left arm slow bowler. Not too quick in the field, but held most of his catches. He had a great rapport with the wicket keeper, who was a good friend, and they had a lot of fun. The ground was very flat, and you could see for miles around. The outfield was baked hard, with thin wiry grass on top. The pavilion was made of bamboo poles and covered with palm leaves. Very little privacy, and was used mainly for cover for food and refreshments, and protection from the sun. There might have been a large upright fridge. In front was a seating area with a couple of small flower beds, and alongside this a cluster of palm trees. These were covered with the hanging nests of weaver birds. Small, very noisy, very busy, very colourful and very beautiful. We loved sitting there with a glass of orange and often bowls of peanuts, baked locally and sprinkled with salt. The cricket was interesting as well.

Servants, we all called them "boys", even though they were usually mature adults. They had a special place in the household. A good head boy was well respected and appreciated. We had Mohamed, a fine upright man who stayed with the family for many years. A lovely person. He was in charge of the boys, and we hardly ever had any trouble. Many years later though, during the Mau Mau difficulties, my father had to rescue him from the chef, a Kikuyu, who had been with us for sometime, but had a knife to his throat. The chef left. Accommodation was supplied by the family, and the jobs were well sought after, and gave a lot of respect in the local community. Mohamed usually wore a loose fitting white cloak, and sometimes a small round peakless cap. We also had an Ayah or nursery maid. As very young children we spent a lot of time with her, and apparently I could speak Swahili before English. She was trusted and liked and also very fond of me. She couldn't get over the fair coloured hairs on my arms and legs and used to call me 'simba', or lion. My natural hair was dark. We acquired a small black kitten. It was very wild. Nobody could get near it, and the boys were not impressed. However over a period of time I did establish a rapport and mutual respect, and fondness.

In the compound was a garden area with some very high trees and bushes. There was a room allocated as a kindergarten classroom close by, and for our breaks and sometimes lessons we would go out there. After a while a family of monkeys inhabited the higher branches, and we used to like watching them. Unfortunately, some residents living nearby complained that their gardens were being raided, and that they were frightened. A number of meetings were called and eventually my father was asked to shoot them, or scare them away. He was known to be a good shot, and possibly the best in the area. He was very reluctant, but eventually agreed on the basis of no risk to the children, including his own. On the day appointed, the class was moved to a room on the river front. If the monkeys appear, sit still where you are, sudden movement could cause a reaction. We could hear some shots from the garden. First up on to her chair was the teacher, closely followed by the class on to their little tables. Synchronisation could not have bettered the process, except one, 'twas I. The monkey stood there on all fours, in the doorway, and just looked at us for a few moments.

The look on his face was one of disappointment and dismay, no fear or aggression, just how could you. Then it turned and disappeared and was never seen again. The class collapsed in chaos, and we had the rest of the day off to recover. However my action had been noted, and I gained a few brownie points. Apparently dad killed one, but we never saw them again. The adults stood about shoulder height to a child. They did steal our lunch boxes once.

They had to go. Rabies was one fear.

The kindergarten was later moved to a bungalow further down the street which was more accessible. There was an occasion when one of the front rooms was used as a store for Army weapons. Rifles, machine guns etc, but I do not recall a sentry, and there was quite a bit of concern about this. Eventually it was removed.

Uncle Eric came to Tanga on embarkation leave. At least, he ended up in hospital with malaria, and I can remember visiting him there. A single storey building, with most rooms opening out onto covered verandas and gardens. He seemed to be recovering, and was being well looked after. He had been seconded to join the Kings African Rifles and was shortly to go to Burma. As children we didn't see much of him, although our parents did. He was tall, well built, very fit, with a good sense of humour, but also very professional, and loved the Army. He was the only member of the family that I can remember with a moustache. The day came for him to go, and I can recall going with dad, to an area that had a large lagoon surrounded by trees. He was dressed in full uniform, with a brown leather belt and diagonal across his chest and looked very smart. There were no buildings, no pier, no send off party, just us. He was ferried out to join a small seaplane. He sat in the rear seat, there was a roar of the engine, a cascade of spray across the water, a wave of the hand and he was away, never to be seen by the family again. He was killed in action. Apparently he was on patrol in the

Pre-war bullock cart

Mum on the flat balcony

Pam and I posing

Dad and us

jungle and became separated from his group. The instructions were, to not attempt to try a rescue. It could be a trap. He was beheaded in the morning. This created problems for me when I traded to Japan a few years later. As a Christian, one has to try to accept and forgive. This was their culture, they didn't know any different, but things have thankfully changed since.

Tanga had a swimming pool. Well more of an area cordoned off by wire netting, and a pontoon forty yards offshore on a site downstream of the port. Alongside was the clubhouse with a large veranda. In front was a sandy beach two yards wide. It was here that I taught myself to swim. I was probably six. I simply found a depth that I felt comfortable in, and on one leg hopped up and down the beach, making swimming motions, until I found that I no longer needed the ground.

You are going to a Boarding School. Oh dear, was I that naughty. My mother always said that I was a little horror. We drove a long way through the plains and bush, and arrived at a travel lodge place in the hills. 'Lussotto'. Much cooler and surrounded by lush green vegetation on the side of valleys. Obviously used for recreation and stopovers. There was a large bungalow building which housed the restaurant, bar and lounge areas, and outside were twenty or so basic chalets. Very pleasant. There was a path down the side of a valley through a kitchen garden which led to a stream at the bottom. Most people seemed to enjoy this, and we found it very exciting. All sorts of possibilities in the foliage. The school was nearby and I was duly taken there. Lovely surroundings, friendly staff, well most of them, and I hated it. Too young. It was here that I was converted from left to right handed, and hours of copying letters didn't improve matters. I also had to sit with a cross tied to my back because I slouched. Still do. I can recall the excitement at the beginning and end of term when the buses, or converted lorries, collected or delivered pupils, usually in the early hours due to the very long distances some had to travel. On one occasion the family came up to take me out for the day. A big treat. All went well until the heavens opened and the roads flooded quickly. Luckily we were near a house and, although we were total strangers we were made very welcome, and dried out in front of a big fire. Food was produced, possibly we had interrupted a party, but it was very spicy and strong tasting for a young palette. In a loud voice I said that it tasted worse than it looked. End of hospitality, profuse apologies, and luckily the rain had stopped. Eventually I was taken away from the school because we were transferring to Mombasa.

We took over a bungalow that belonged to the Harbour Master, Bill Reed, who was away, but a good friend of dad's. We met him briefly, short, plump, bachelor, and obviously enjoyed to socialise. The house was in its own grounds with a large overgrown open area at the back, which had a pathway through the middle often used by the locals. One day there was a bad bush fire there, which luckily stopped at our fence, but it did drive a lot of wildlife out and into our garden, including a lot of snakes. The boys had quite a lot of fun chasing and killing them, and there were a few dead reptiles. When the excitement subsided, I went out and rode my tricycle over them. The boys thought this was great fun. The reptiles were of different colours, and most about three foot long. On another occasion my mother called me into the back bedroom and pointed to the flower bed. There, wending its way through the plants was a brown snake about four foot long with a small head, my immediate reaction was to call the boys, but she said no, and we watched it for a few minutes before it returned to the bush. I resolved not to go over the fence to retrieve toys etc. Six year olds can be very wise you know. On another occasion there was some excitement in the orchard next door, there was a six foot python in the trees, but they wouldn't let me near.

Dad was acting as Agent for many ships, including the Royal Navy. He had been enlisted into the KAR, but was quickly seconded out to continue his duties. This involved arranging stores, mail, doctors etc. and we were invited on to a Greek freighter for dinner. This was very interesting.

The Far Eastern fleet was due, very hush hush. We went up to the heads to see the ships in, and dad was most perturbed because of all the onlookers already there. So much for security.

The harbour has a narrow entrance which opens out into a broad lagoon. There is a ferry across, and on one occasion I had made friends with an African boy who had a small canoe with out-riggers. That was great fun. Lots of jellyfish though.

Mombasa was very hot and humid, but with some lovely beaches nearby. On one occasion I can remember slipping and hitting my mouth very hard on the steep stone steps. I was convinced that that is what affected my front teeth. The experts say not.

TROOPSHIP

1944

We joined the troopship *Nea Hellas* in Mombasa, and sailed 28-6-44. I was aged 7.

She was painted in grey camouflage, bristled with anti aircraft guns, and a six inch gun on the poop. Apparently she had seen a lot of service in the war, which was not yet over, and I think she was carrying a lot of wounded from the Far East, but we didn't see these until they disembarked in Glasgow.

Boat drill was held immediately, as is normal, and we duly paraded in grossly oversized lifejackets. Pam recalls that the seafarers hymn was always played on these occasions. 'Eternal Father'. This is still a favourite of mine. The lifeboat painters were always secured ready for use, and hung in great loops along the ship's side, swinging out, and clunking back in as the ship rolled. Our cabin was internal, hot, airless, noisy, and we bathed in salt water.

We were unescorted, and one evening they decided to set off outdated distress fireworks, which was great fun, but at the time I felt was a bit risky and there was no attempt at a blackout. Possibly there were escorts out of sight. Recently I have learnt that German and Jap U-boats were in the area, and on 28-8-44 sank an American freighter off Oman.

We stopped at Aden for bunkers. Very barren, very rocky, very hot.

Eventually we arrived at Port Suez, anchored, were fitted with a searchlight on the bow, and in due course joined the canal convoy.

This was very exciting. The desert sands came right to the edge of the waterway. A road, a railway, a freshwater canal all ran along one side, with occasional oasis of trees, camels, donkeys. It was here it was discovered that I had German measles, the first of many. I was taken into the hospital which was on the poop, and directly under a battery of guns. We anchored in the Bitter Lakes as is normal, to let the southbound convoy through, and many crew and passengers had a swim. Then some idiot decided to have gun practice, and I wasn't feeling very well. Metal to metal, bang to bang, even the shell cases made a hell of a clatter when they hit the metal deck. Life seemed very quiet afterwards. The nursing staff, which included a number of men, were very good and attentive. The ward quickly filled up, about 8 of us, and other rooms were requisitioned. Many people were affected with the outbreak.

We continued our passage north, I don't remember much of this, it could have been night, but I do remember the Johnny Walker sign lit up at Port Said. 'Born 1879 & Still going strong'. We anchored outside, and over the next couple of days the convoy steadily built up with what seemed like hundreds of ships of all shapes and sizes, and small escort vessels dashing all over the place. We set sail and the ships took up their positions. We were in the middle, it was a big convoy and ships stretched to the horizon, it was possibly one of the last convoys of the war.

Occasionally we could see larger escort vessels. No enemy planes, but there was a strong rumour that a submarine had been seen and dealt with. After a while I was up and about, and on one occasion I was shown how to work the big six inch gun, and pointed it at nearby ships. This rather concerned me, as I didn't want them to get the wrong impression.

Soon I was discharged, there seemed be a lot of people waiting to be admitted, including a number of adults, and I felt very sorry, that after what a lot had been through, that they had been knocked over by my measles. Shipboard life continued, the weather was pleasant, boat drills, another gunnery practice, which I did enjoy this time, as I could see what was going on, and wasn't so close to the 'Pom poms, bofors, oerlicans' etc, all belting away.

Some enthusiasts were trying to set up a concert. The ship only had two useable records left. There was little else to do.

On one occasion I was playing on deck with some lead soldiers that I had been given. One had become separated and was only a few feet away. I left it there, as it was quiet, after a while an Army officer strolled by, saw it, stopped, picked it up, stared at it for a few moments, and then hurled it as far out to sea as he could. I didn't say anything, as I sensed that soldiering and war meant something far different to him.

After a while it started to get cooler, windier, and then wetter. We arrived at Glasgow and went alongside. It was summer, 11-8-44, and we couldn't' get used to the late light nights. We watched whilst many wounded and patients were discharged, and eventually we boarded a troop train. It was packed to busting. We found ourselves at the end of a corridor and on the floor. We all settled down for the night. A Wren very kindly offered her lap for my head, and I thought that this was a very nice arrangement. Unfortunately some idiot found a seat for us. Space for one, so we ended up sitting upright, and very squashed. Penzance was a very very long way. We arrived late evening, it was still light. We alighted straight on to the tracks and had to carry our luggage. Kenya seemed a long way away.

Grandad in East Africa, 1911

John on duty, Khano

ENGLAND

1944-1946

We were transferred in a very large black taxi to Tuckingmill Vicarage. It was late, we were very tired. I recall a large ivy covered building in its own grounds, surrounded by high hedges, and with a tall tree growing out of the lawn. We were made very welcome by Aunty Win, as the others were away. We soon went to bed. It was still light. As sometimes happens when you are very tired, I couldn't sleep. I can remember going to the window, to make sure that there weren't any snakes crawling up the ivy. One didn't encourage that sort of growth in Africa.

Next day we met Grandad. He was the Vicar. A tall imposing man, athletic in his day, well respected, but we loved him, even if he was a bit remote at times. He had a twin identical brother Bill, who was Rector of Lydd Church in Kent throughout the war, directly under the path of the Battle of Brittain air fights, and the doodle bugs.

Granny was his second wife, a slim, loving, educated and very efficient woman, the family organiser and letter writer. Auntie Dolly was her younger sister - smaller, a spinster, a great helper and a bustling type of woman. There was never any mention of male involvement. Possibly this was a legacy of the First World War. They were in the WRVS, and did a lot of community work. They would often disappear to give tea to the troops.

Auntie Win was Grandad's sister. Spinster, tall and slim, highly educated, very imposing. She had been Headmistress of Reading College, and also taught Latin. She had bought shares in Premier Polish from an ex pupil, when it was first started.

Uncle Bill was married to Auntie Con. She was a very strong,

*Tim and Rosemary's
engagement*

*John, Rosemary,
Auntie Win and Eric*

rebellious and vivacious character. They had three children. Pru was the eldest and very independent. She became involved with the entertainment world, and married Peter Myers, a very successful BBC producer. They had three children. Sadly this ended in divorce, but she later married Oliver Postgate. Enter 'Bagpuss' and 'Nogin the Nog'. She occasionally wrote to us, was very friendly, and there was an open invitation for us to go and visit. Sadly we weren't able to do so. The latest manual appeared at Christmas. This was always appreciated. Capel was his own man. A bachelor, who worked in the management team of BR, in London. He was pleasant to get on with, and had a very dry sense of humour. Paul was the youngest. He always wanted to be a Vicar. I met him a few times, and he was probably the easiest to get on with. He met Clem, who he later married, and he ended up as a Canon in Winchester Cathedral. He introduced me to Jim Payne, who was a newly appointed Mission to Seamen Padre in Liverpool.

We soon settled into the vicarage routine, there were two evacuee families staying there, but they soon went home. There was a farm at the back, which I loved to go to, to watch milking very early in the morning, and I was always made very welcome, Vicar's Grandson you know. The Cornish are like that.

Blackberry picking was a very important occasion. The whole family went. Rationing was still in force, but we seemed to eat well. There were seven of us in the house. There was a kitchen garden at the back, like most houses, and it was well stocked. High tea was a main event. This consisted of a small hot dish, followed by bread and jam, or honey. Dripping was a popular dish.

Soon it was Christmas. There was a Parish Nativity Play.

On Christmas morning, at 6am, there was a clatter of metallic music from the hall. The local campanologists had decided to give the household a surprise treat. They succeeded, and it was very good. Very quickly we put on our dressing gowns, and enjoyed the show. Soon it was time for tea and mince pies, and the grown ups went to 8am communion. Breakfast was always afterwards. Stockings were opened, and much excitement ensued. We all went to the 11am service. There were a few visitors, but we then had a family present opening session. This led on to the full Christmas Lunch, with all the trimmings. We ate well in Tanga, but there were some limitations. There is nothing like a proper English Christmas meal well cooked. After the Queen's speech, things quietened down. Tea and traditional cake were served in the drawing room. The evening was more informal, and we soon found ourselves playing party games. Charades, murder, donkey, I Spy, hunt the thimble. Good atmosphere and fun. A lovely day.

Boxing Day, and families tended to go out for a walk, or visiting. Life continued for a while, but it was felt that Pam and I needed education.

Arrangements were made for us to go to 'Roscrow', a small boarding, kindergarten school, near Falmouth. This was a large country house with ample grounds, in a lovely setting. It was owned by, and run by the 'Farrant' family. Dad was away in the RN. A Lieutenant. We only saw him once, and his party trick was to jump over a bar at shoulder height, from a standing start. This was duly demonstrated.

Mum ran the school, and her elderly mother, who was probably the owner, also chipped in. There were about a dozen pupils including their son, and a few regular staff. This included a young, early 20s, unsympathetic Scottish female teacher. She was not well liked by us. The food was good, and there was a very large kitchen garden. The head gardener was a retired RN Chief Petty Officer, and took the boys for sport. He taught us the rudiments of boxing, and was very good. There was an outbuilding that housed a number of rabbits. We were all allocated a hutch to look after, and we enjoyed that, but Pam and I were not happy, and did not enjoy our time there. On Sundays we would be taken to different local churches, which I did like, and on VE day we were taken to some cliffs where we could see the beaches, and rejoicings in Falmouth. We didn't stay too late. A joyful time. Roscrow was later taken over by some Nuns, and has now been converted to upmarket apartments.

Whilst this was going on, our future was being discussed. Beaumont House was considered for me, following Uncle Eric's impressions. So I went there for a couple of terms.

Everywhere was dull and grey. Recovery from the war years had not yet started. Rationing was still in force, there were shortages. Troops were still away, and families were still split up. There was a lot of uncertainty.

RETURN TO NAIROBI

1946-1947

We travelled to Southampton to join the RMS *Alcantara*. She was a Royal Mail Steamship vessel, but had been seconded to help replace lost tonnage, and to get people moving again. She had two yellow funnels, was newer, and at 18 knots was faster than the others. She carried about 200 passengers, and had been a troopship during the war. The passage was uneventful, but it was strange to be in an empty ocean, and not surrounded by other ships.

When we arrived in Mombasa, we were taken to a hotel for an overnight stay, whilst the baggage was unloaded. I remember thatched roofs and bungalows on the beach, and a large swimming pool. Some friends came to greet Mum. Friendships in the Colonies were very strong and enduring.

Next day we joined the overnight sleeper to Nairobi. What an experience. We had our own compartment. This had a seat, which at night was converted into two bunk beds. There was a small wash basin. There was no air conditioning, so the window had to be kept open, even at night. However there was a mosquito screen that could be positioned. The track went straight out into the bush and scrubland. Wild animals were all over the place, and wandering around. Giraffes, zebras, antelope, gazelles, even lion in the distance. It was a magical ever changing scene. The train was climbing steadily, so it wasn't very fast. The sunset and twilight were beautiful, even to a 10 year old. We all slept well, and in the morning arrived at Voi. There were dozens of people selling fruit and other local wares, and we all disembarked to stretch our legs, clean up, and to breakfast. Almost a holiday atmosphere. The train was cleaned and restored to day use, and the engine took on water. Lots of it. The engine was huge, a

Garrett. This meant that the main boiler was suspended between two large water tanks. The wheels were not as large as in UK, and the fuel was wood. Strong and sturdy, rather than fast. We duly set off, and carried on climbing. Occasionally we would slow down, even stop, to allow locals to hop on to two flat trucks at the back. You don't often see Masai warriors in full regalia, including spears, hopping on to the morning commute to Charing Cross. Eventually, in the late afternoon we arrived at Nairobi station. There was Dad, dressed in smart white shirt and shorts, and long stockings. He always dressed well. Terrific welcome and family reunion. We were together again.

He drove us to a nice company bungalow in a pleasant suburb on the outskirts of Nairobi. The front was on the top of a low hill, with lovely views of the Ngong Hills in the distance. These changed colour during the day, from a light brown in the morning, to a purplish hue in the evening. The back garden dropped away into three terraces. The bottom one was barren and untouched, but the other two were grassed, and were perfectly adequate for cricket and other activities. The windows had metal security grids. There had been a lot of thefts, and as there was no air conditioning, windows were left open at night. Even so, gangs would use long poles with a hook on the end, to fish out handbags and things. They were known as 'pole fishers'.

Dad kept working, and we gradually settled in. Sadly, the parental rows intensified, and became more frequent. We knew that things were not right. There was a pleasant Christmas, and some nice letters from Granny and others at home. They had grown apart. Not surprising with the long absences, different life styles, war effects, and tropical conditions. Dad loved the job and life, and was doing well. Mum had very strong views on education, and was determined that we would be educated in England.

Pam and I both went to the Nairobi High School. A very large school which was split into Junior, Middle and Senior sections. The weather could be very pleasant. Nairobi is about 5,000 feet above sea level, so it was very hot during the day, but cooler at night. The 'wet,' or 'monsoon' seasons were March to May. The Headmaster and his wife were both very tubby, and they drove around in a small pre-war Morris car. We wondered how they had got in, and if one was on their own, it would lean over quite alarmingly. Such is the observation of 10 year olds. Discipline was very strict, but usually fair. One of my teachers was a Mrs McMurdo. Shortish, with ginger hair, and a quick temper. Any infringements would be followed by a whack, or two, using the class gym shoe. One day it was me. The instrument of torture could not be found. I was the only one wearing gym shoes. So I had to solemnly remove a shoe, and punishment was duly administered, but by this time the venom had subsided, the blows were softer, and we all found it to be highly amusing. She was actually a good teacher. Another teacher would show his displeasure by hurling the wooden blackboard wiper. You were safest if he was looking at you. Dad would collect us at the end of the afternoon. On one occasion, I was called out of lunch, and told to go home for a dental appointment. I knew nothing about this, and queried it, but I was told to go. So I packed up and set off for home, a few miles away. It was very hot. It was a long and dusty road, and I walked past gangs of convicts working on the roadside, with an 'Askari' guard in attendance. They looked at me, I looked at them and kept walking. Was I an absconder? Eventually I arrived at home, and my Mother was horrified. She knew nothing about any appointment. Dad was very distressed when they couldn't find me when he went to the school as normal. Of course, it all came out, another clerical mistake. Sport was very important, and cricket the most popular. Dad did a lot of coaching with the Seniors. He was a member of three clubs, Nairobi, Muthaiga, and the Kongoni's. The latter was a strong touring side with no ground, but they had a lot of fun, and we loved going to the away matches.

A Manager's house was being built in Muthaiga, an upmarket district of Nairobi. The divorce proceedings were in progress. During the summer holidays, Pam and I were sent to a farm which catered for children vacations. This was run by the farm manager, Lennox and his wife. They were childless, but loved kids. There were about a dozen of us, and we had a wonderful time. It was a large sprawling farm, and we got involved with the animals. Lennox would take us for sporting activities, and he tried to teach me to catch a ball. With a tennis racket he would hit it as high as he could. I became quite good, and he would give me a small prize if I held 100 without a drop. There were a number of times when I got into the high 90s. Great fun, and I was always a good catcher.

Eventually we returned, but to Muthaiga. Mum had moved to a flat in the City, and had a job. Joyce moved in as Dad's partner. She was a nurse, very professional and a good socialiser. We thought that she was a rather hard uncaring woman. We got on, but there was no feeling. She had been married before, and had travelled a lot, including China. Mohamed was still the Head boy.

The house was near the top of a gentle hill, and the ground dropped away to a small stream at the bottom. About an acre in total. The road at the top was fairly flat, and there were a number of other families who had just moved in, so we soon made a number of friends. We all had bikes, and spent many hours pottering around. Our closest were the Goodwins, two sons of our age. There was a house being built between our homes, and we borrowed some of the stones to build a small den. We were warned to check for snakes, seeking a shelter, whenever we went in. Never saw one. Years later, I heard that their Dad had been killed when a pistol in his pocket had gone off. Possibly it had become cocked accidentally. It was the time of the Mau Mau difficulties. There was an occasion when the boys said they had found a snake skin in our garden, probably a cobra. I of course went to investigate, but thankfully found nothing. Dad created a garden area at the bottom near the stream. So we had some good veg.

It was a large house with two stories. Upstairs had three bedrooms, with the master having an en-suite. There was also a bathroom and toilet. The passage led on to a balcony and stairs, which led into a very large lounge. Joyce loved Siamese cats, and had two. Ba Ba and Mei Mei. The floors were wooden, and on one occasion Ba Ba chased along the passage, braked, skidded and flew into the lounge and landed on the settee. Once we had established that he was OK, we collapsed with laughter. Funnily enough, he never did that again. Downstairs was the kitchen and pantry, and a large dining room. Near the top of the wall ran a plate rail. The cats would chase around this when we were having our tea. Thankfully there were no plates.

The divorce had now gone through, and Mum had custody of us. We were allowed to read the local papers, but it was noticeable that many passages had been cut out. There was talk of a baby on the way. Arrangements were made for us to return to England. Afraid it had a negative social effect on all of them, as it did in those days.

We duly joined the SS *Modasa* in Mombasa, a medium sized cargo passenger ship, which carried about a 100 passengers. Practical rather than luxurious. She was owned by the British India Steam Packet, who also ran regular services to East Africa. She had a black hull, white superstructure, and a funnel that had two horizontal white stripes. Very distinctive. There was a pleasant relaxed atmosphere on board, and the voyage was uneventful. We called at Aden for bunkers, and we were able to go ashore to see Pam's Godfather, Dan Crawshaw, who was the Governor. We also visited Port Sudan. The land of the 'Fuzzy Wuzzies'. That's what we kids called the locals, who all seemed to have heads that were covered with large bushy hair. Almost like wigs. It was a very hot, flat, desert and sandy sort of place, but we were able to go in a glass bottomed boat out to the coral reefs. What colours, what an experience.

The ship anchored in Plymouth Sound. It was a grey day with a light breeze and slight swell. A pontoon was placed alongside, and baggage was loaded into a tender. This then took us ashore. We journeyed to Penzance, where the whole family came to greet us. Thus ended my fourth voyage, I was 10.

PENZANCE

1947-1949

Grandad had now been moved to St Paul's Church in Penzance. This was near the Farmer's Market, and he would love to tell potential visitors to go to the Pig Market, and then ask for the Vicar. The vicarage was a short walk away, and was the end terrace of a very large imposing block. This was three stories high, with a large basement. We were allocated the top floor. You could see over the houses, with a lovely view of St Michael's Bay. St Michael's Mount to the left, and sweeping round to the fishing port of Newlyn to the right. You could make out where Mousehole was. Occasionally you could see a basking shark in the distance. However, it was very exposed, and would rattle and shake during the gales. As children we were allowed to use the basement, and spread out our toys. This included my Hornby train set, Meccano, and Pam's prams and dolls. There was a bakery immediately behind at the back, and this would wake us all up at 5 am, when they started baking. Lovely bread and rolls though. There was a lawn area which stretched the length of the building, with a narrow road around the edge. So the children had space to play and kick balls. Very safe.

Pam and I would wander around and explore all over the place. This included the harbour and seawall, where we would often watch the 'Scillonian' being loaded and discharged. She was the purpose built ferry to the Isles of Scilly. A very robust looking vessel. We were very disturbed kids though, and we would shout and yell at each other. Deep down we were great friends, and I suppose this was our way of getting the mixed up emotions out of the system. There would be family outings St Ives, Mousehole, Lands End, and to the 'Warspite'. This was a very famous battleship, which had broken adrift when she was being towed to the breakers yard, and had stranded near Praa sands. People were very saddened at the undignified end to a war icon. Pam started at a local school, and arrangements were made for me to return to Beaumont House for the winter term of 1947.

This involved catching the 'Cornish Riviera' from Penzance. The World famous GWR Express. 360 miles in 360 minutes. Do they do that now? Everybody was very proud of this, and she was very rarely late. Every boy, and many adults, would have to go and see which engine was taking you. King George Vth, King Henry, and King Edward being regulars. I would be taken to a 3rd Class apartment, clutching my sandwiches. Much hissing of steam, smoke, whistles, doors banging, and you were away. A slow, but very powerful pull away, but then she would get into her stride. Much rattling and swaying, but what power and speed, and the countryside racing by. Always thrilling, but you had to be careful with which windows were open, because the smoke would soon come in, and very often there was soot in it. Not good for the eyes if you stuck your head out of the corridor windows, as any self-respecting 10 to 14 year old would do. The train would stop and load up in most of the Cornish stations, and then at Exeter, Taunton, other main line stops, and on to Paddington. The first couple of times I was accompanied, but then did it on my own both ways, but always the family would come down to send me off, or to welcome me back. The Guard would be asked to keep an eye on me, and I never had any problems. In fact I loved the trust. Because of the luggage, I would have to get a taxi to Marylebone station, where we would be met by a Master, and meet up with most of the other pupils. Who has left, who is staying on, what news, much excitement. The train would be a stopper to Chorleywood. The compartments were boxes, usually smelly and grimy, and it would be dark outside, and dim inside. Taxis would take us to the school. Hot chocolate, big helloes and welcome, and back to your dormitories. Most of us were very tired.

St Paul's was a very busy parish with a good choir, and Grandad was well respected. He was made a Canon in Truro diocese. The Mousehole Male Voice Choir came to do a concert, and I can remember intense conversations about what was suitable to sing in a church. How things have changed now. They were very good. Sadly Grandad died in 1949 aged 67. Family and parish mourning took over. We all missed him. Pam and I did not go to the funeral.

It was now all change. A Vicarage is a working building, and we would have to make way for the next incumbent. There is usually a time lag, so there was no rush, but we all had to get on with it. Granny and her sisters moved out and stayed with friends, and later bought a house in Worthing. Carrick Beg, an Irish name reflecting their family ancestry. Auntie Rosie joined them later. The elder sister. She was a lovely and sweet lady. She was more worldly than the other two, and obviously had the cash. She was the widow of a vicar, George Baskerville, who also had been involved as a missionary in East Africa, mostly in Uganda. During the war, they were living in the Channel Islands, and were told to stay there, and liaise with the occupying Germans. Not an easy task.

Mum started to find jobs at boarding schools as an Assistant Matron, where we could live and stay during the holidays. She would take over whilst the regular staff were away. It worked very well, and she did stints at St Michaels in Limpsfield, Surrey, Beaumont House, and then High Trees School near Horley in Surrey. We had bags of space and freedom, to wander around, or cycle. Sometimes we would house sit in Worthing during the summer holidays, so that the Aunts could go and stay with friends. We would look after the cat, 'Ossie'. He was a lovely tom, with shiny jet black hair, but with a very distinct white bib and white paws. Of course the beach was quite close. We had to put food leftovers into a disgusting pigswill bin, for the farmers to collect. We also had some holidays at Beddingham in Sussex. This was a converted school house in a small hamlet in the South Downs. A lovely spot. It was owned by a family friend, Auntie Ruth. She was very sweet, who lived with her close friend Miss Sprigg. She was quite a hard, but a fair person, and had been in the WRENS during the war. They had a terrier Paddy, he was great fun. The small church was across the road, and they were very involved with that. We had some lovely Easters there, and the weather was always gorgeous. We got to know some of the local farmers and their children, and would visit their farms. Walks onto the Downs, with the cowslips, were always popular. Sometimes we would come across disused hand grenades, where the troops had been exercising. We were always very careful. On one occasion the sky was filled, horizon to horizon, with bombers going on one of the last big raids of the war. They took a long time to pass over.

BEAUMONT HOUSE

1947-1951

Set on a low hill in delightful countryside a few miles from Rickmansworth and Chorleywood, in Hertfordshire, it was at the end of a very long, rough, unadopted lane, which had some very nice detached properties, and high hedges, on each side. The grounds were over eight acres, which included a swimming pool, sports pitches, tennis court, and a large market garden with orchards.

Beaumont House was a private Preparatory Boarding School, with about 60 pupils. Most were boarding. The education was built around the Common Entrance exam, for entry to the major Public Schools. It was very much a home from home, but with strict discipline, and a strong Christian and outdoor ethos. Many of the boys came from well to do families in the Home Counties, but there were also some colonial boys, and the two sons of Jack Jackson, the well known broadcaster and band leader. He lived in Denham a few miles away, and close to the film studios. These were contemporaries of mine. The elder, John, was Head boy when I rejoined in the winter term of 1947.

Mr P H Vezey was the owner and Headmaster. He had been one time Inspector of schools in Nigeria. He was a tall imposing, very fit man, with a distinctive silvery grey moustache, and a shiny head. His wife, Joanna, was younger and very good looking, but we felt that she tended to be more in the background. After a while they had a daughter, Judith.

Mr Vezey, or Pedro as we nicknamed him, had taken over in 1941 from Mr Keating. There was talk of cash problems, probably made worse by war conditions, so Vezey got a good price, but there was some bitterness. Having said that, I can recall seeing his son, Harry, the crime author, having exclusive use of the nets to hone up his fast bowling skills. It was about that time when my Uncle Eric had done his short stint as a teacher.

A typical day would start about 0700. We would all go out to the parade ground, and the Head Boy would lead us in PT exercises. The occasional Master would wander past, but rarely interfered. We would then go and clean up, and to breakfast at 0800. Cereal or porridge, and followed by a hot dish of bacon and egg, or kipper, or yellow fish. Toast afterwards. We would then clean our teeth, make our beds, and proceed to the toilets. Here matron, a Miss Jones, would wait patiently, and we would tell her if we had done a number one or number two. This was entered into her exercise book. Two days negative, and you attended sick parade for syrup of figs. She was a very strict woman, without much humour. However I did get to know her later, and found her to be a very nice person. No mention of any male involvement, but this could have been a legacy of the 1st World War. Not many males left.

After this, one had free time and we could wander around, play ball, and chat. There was a short 9 hole golf course around the edge of the playing fields, and many of us would use it. You could choose a club from a selection of oddments, none from the same set. My favourite was a 3 iron with a wooden shaft, which became a pitcher, putter, or driver as required. Great fun. At 0900 the Head Boy would strike the bell at the end of a passage, call 'All In' outside as loudly as possible. This was the signal for boys and Masters to go to the Morning Assembly in the gymnasium. The pupils were divided into four houses, A B C D, and sat in age seniority around the sides. The eldest being the leader. The attendance would be checked, and when your name was called, you responded 'adsum'. Latin for 'I am here'. The Headmaster would then lead with a couple of prayers, a hymn, short Bible reading, and a short talk. Any announcements, and then each house leader would pass down his team, and any stars or demerits would be declared. There were 4 coloured lines painted on the wooden wall, a large coloured hat pin would be moved up or down, and the success of the sections was clearly visible. I was in A, and our colour was orange. We usually did quite well.

We would have one or two lessons before a break, and then one after, up to lunch. The subjects were: Maths, Latin, English, French, History, Geography, and Scripture. There were 3 classrooms in the main block, and these had solid fuel stoves. No central heating. The senior class was in the end room of a large a wooden hut. This had 2 or three paraffin heaters as required. It was still very cold in there.

Lunch would be a two course hot meal. This would be followed by 2 more lessons, with a break in between. There would then be outside activities, or gym if the weather was unkind. On Wednesdays and Saturdays there would be games, and no afternoon classes. Soccer, cricket, athletics, swimming, or rugby in season. In extreme weather there would be gym, boxing, and sometimes black and white films shown in the gym, including a fairly recent Pathe News report. One report showed the opening up of the Belsen POW camp. Mr Vezey thought hard before showing this, and we were duly very saddened at what we saw. We thought he was right to show it. Sporting Internationals were always popular.

For those who were unable to participate in the games on medical grounds, there was the sick parade, or walking wounded as they were named. Jobs would be allocated in the garden or orchard, depending on season and one's actual fitness. These included, pruning, weeding, fruit picking, mowing and garden chores generally. These were usually allocated by Mr Vezey, but were very often with the gardener. He was an interesting character. He lived on his own in a wooden Romany caravan at the far end of the estate. He knew his nature, and was highly

100 yards flyer

*Pavillion and
school, 1950*

regarded and respected. Because of my knee, I spent a lot of time in this group, and learnt to respect and love nature. We were almost self-sufficient. Boys were also offered a small flower bed to look after, and help and encouragement was always available.

At 1800 the evening meal would be a High Tea with a hot dish, soup, or an egg on toast type of thing, and bread and jam. Tea would be served in glasses, and this is where we learnt to put a metal spoon in first, to stop cracking and disintegration.

There would be an hour's prep, and then this would be followed by supervised activities and hobbies. Slide shows, cigarette cards, post cards, readings, photography, stamp collections, letter writing. Occasionally there would be talks by a boy, and gentle debates. Bed time would be about 2200.

Letter writing was taken very conscientiously. This was our chance to keep our folk in touch with what we were doing, our successes, our disappointments, and we felt that we were still very much part of our family. Many members would be involved, and we appreciated their replies. Many were separated by huge distances. In my case my Father was in Kenya, and the weekly letter eagerly anticipated. My Uncle and Godfather were in Nigeria, and we corresponded regularly every four years, but I knew that he was there. When he was home on leave, he always made a point of taking me out for the day. He also had appreciated boarding school.

Sundays were special. A leisurely morning, before the whole school trooped off to St Johns church at the far end of the lane in Heronsgate, for the 10.30 morning service. The lane was unadopted, and it was very rough and rutted. Bad weather did not stop us, and we were well wrapped up. We all sat at the back and sang lustily. The attendance was good, considering the catchment area, and I enjoyed the services. It was here, during some of the sermons, that I started thinking about what I was going to do. Memories of what I had seen, and done, on my travels became dominant. That's when I decided that I wanted to go to sea. My academic ability hardly justified thinking of going to one of the prestigious Public Schools.

Sunday lunch was always special. Rationing was still in operation, but the school had plenty of fresh fruit and veg. Mr Vezey would pick out interesting articles from the *Sunday Times*, match reports, and of course the football results. No Final Score then. The Head Boy would collect his bottle of beer for him. Later in the afternoon the Duty Master would take us on a ramble. Each time in a different direction, and interesting nature would be pointed out. A pleasant time to chat and wander around, even pick wild mushrooms in season. It always seemed to be sunny then. On one occasion we came across some netting to trap birds, this was quickly and unceremoniously taken down and destroyed.

After tea, the boarders would collect their 'tuck', and meet in Mr Vezey's lounge. We would make ourselves comfy, and he would read a passage to us from a pre-chosen book, usually Rudyard Kipling. A time to relax and reflect. Sweets were still rationed, so the boys would indicate what they wanted, and a senior boy would go to an approved sweet shop, to collect the goodies. This would be handed to the matron, and she would distribute later. On one occasion I was sent on this mission. As I didn't have a bike, I had to borrow one. Luckily I was offered a very new modern vehicle which had a 3 speed. When I came out of the shop, I was surrounded by 5 local youths on bikes, who indicated that they thought that we were trumped up 'toffs'. Naturally I was in school uniform. We set off. Thankfully I was able to slow them right down until they wobbled and lost balance. By this time I was in top gear, and able to accelerate away. By the time they regained control, I was well away and going down hill. They acknowledged my manoeuvre, but it could have turned nasty. I was aged 12.

In the Summer Term of 1949, my section head, M P I French,

and I, were summoned to the Headmaster's study. Neither of us had any inkling as to why, and we were close friends. We were informed that a new Headboy would be needed for the winter term, and that I was to be appointed. He said some nice things to French, and I was shocked. There were a number of more senior boys than me, and I hadn't even thought that I was being considered. This decision was duly announced in Assembly, and I moved up to the top seat. Everybody was surprised, including some of the Masters, but thankfully French and I remained good friends, and he was very supportive.

As Headboy, I was one of the biggest boys in the school, I was fit and good at sport, including boxing, and I think that I got on well with everybody. Apart from the morning exercises, and 'All In', I also had to inspect the boy's hands and faces before meals, and then say the Latin Grace. *'Benedictus benedecat periasum christum dominum nostrum'*. Nobody has ever interpreted this for me.

Sports Days were always special. Masters and boys all helped with the preparations, and the grounds looked terrific. Many parents would come to make a day of it, with picnics and blankets etc. Lovely atmosphere. Unfortunately my knee trouble, Schlatters disease, which resulted in 3 months in plaster, meant that I missed most physical activity during my last two years at BH. This included cricket, football and athletics. Sadly, I would have been Captain of cricket, football and probably rugby. However, as head of my section, I was able to collect the winnings of my team. However, I did have the success of winning, surprisingly, the 100 yards when I was 12. Time 13.6secs. Mr Vezey was very proud of this photo. I was fast and strong, but not expected to win. After an indifferent start, I was determined not to be left behind, and stormed through to win. Prize Giving was a special event, and appreciated by everybody. This was usually finished off with the Big Plunge. All the boys, in group order, would jump into the pool, making

*Prizes and
tug of war*

as big a splash as possible. Non-participants were of course, well soaked.

The swimming pool was always popular, 25 yards long, surrounded by high fences, which helped to keep the winds off. There would of course be the annual swimming gala. Everybody participated, irrespective of standard. A few, well wrapped up, parents would be present. Swimming was taken very seriously, and efforts were made to teach all the boys. Individual abilities were fostered. Afraid I still hate diving. During the winter, if water was still in the pool, there would be sessions, when you could sail your model boats and yachts.

There was a 25 yard shooting range. This had to be paid for, and thankfully Dad did the honours. Mr Vezey always took control, and gun safety was paramount. We were well instructed. There were two boards and two .22 rifles. We learnt a lot, and I became quite good. My claim to fame was when a Father's Day cricket match was abandoned because of rain. It was decided to adjourn to the range, and shoot against each other. My opponent was Jack Jackson. He was very friendly, and it was good fun. He of course beat me, just.

Arrangements were in hand for me to apply to join HMS *Conway*. This was a specialist pre-sea Training Ship, moored in the Menai Straits in North Wales. Mum took me up to Truro Council to sit a Scholarship exam, and we were later awarded with about 30%. Cash was beginning to tighten up, and it wasn't a local school.

In the spring of 1950 I went up to Bangor to attend an interview and sit an Entrance Exam. Here I did quite well, and was subsequently accepted. There seemed to be lots of people around, and we didn't have much chance to see our intended destination. However, in the background there was a change of command. The new Superintendent, Capt. E Hewitt, decided that I would be too young, and deferred my starting for 12 months. This caused some problems and re thinking, but I think that he was right.

Normally you did a couple of terms as Headboy, but I was the youngest to be appointed, and the deferment meant that I would have to do 2 years, so I was also the longest serving. Sadly this of course meant blocking other hopefuls. We could never understand why I was promoted. There were some very influential families there. Was I, the outsider, a tactical choice? If one of the other favourites had been selected, would some of the other parents have been upset?

Speech made on retirement of PH Vezey:

In November 1971 certain Old Boys, as explained later, sent out the following circular letter:

"After more than a year of uncertainty when no one could be sure whether or not Beaumont House was going to continue, the decision has now been taken and the school has finally been closed.

For six generations of boys, or over thirty years, Mr. Vezey has built up a proud and honourable tradition which has made the name of Beaumont House School respected not only in the local community of Chorleywood, but also in the wider academic world of the Public Schools to which the boys moved on.

We all remember Mr. Vezey and no doubt each of us has particular memories, but there are general memories which we all must share. We have all benefitted from his strict sense of discipline, but we all became aware that this was tempered by a genuine Christian kindliness and his standards were accepted by us because we realised that Mr. Vezey practised what he preached.

The time has now come for Mr. Vezey to retire; it may have been comparatively easy for us to leave Beaumont House, but for Mr. Vezey his departure must have been poignant and sad.

As a small token of our appreciation, it is proposed to make a presentation to Mr. Vezey on behalf of all the Old Boys and we feel sure that you would wish to participate. If you do, please send a donation however small. The formal presentation will be made on Sunday, 27th February 1972 at Beaumont House, and anyone who can come will be most welcome. In any event, the names of every contributor will be inscribed and presented to Mr. Vezey on that occasion."

A splendid gathering, for which some Old Boys had travelled very considerable distances, duly met together on the 27th February. For the occasion Mr. Vezey had arranged all the class-rooms and dormitories with desks, beds, chairs etc. set out just as they had been when the school had been fully functioning. Not unnaturally, conversations between old friends went on and on, while it was remarkable how well the various age groups blended, until J. C. Jackson (Head Boy 1947) called the meeting to order and introduced Anthony Abadjian who reported on the business side of the occasion. John Jackson then called on Eden Mathews (Head Boy 1949-51) who spoke as follows:

'Mr. Vezey, Ladies and Gentlemen, and Fellow Old Boys,

I consider it a privilege to be allowed to say a few words to you on this occasion, to mark the retirement of Mr. Vezey. Like most Old Boys, I have always been full of good intentions to visit the school and see Mr. Vezey, possibly a Sports Day or an Old Boys match or something, but regrettably like most Old Boys, I have never actually made it, apart from one short visit just after I had left. I suppose one gets married, moves away and intends to make the visit next summer or may be next year or maybe, well anyway the result is always mañana. For my sins, living in Shropshire, I plead distance. Nevertheless, it came as a bit of a shock to receive the letter from the committee last November advising me that not only was Mr. Vezey mortal and has to retire some time, but also that the school has had to close as well. It came as a bigger shock to realise that it is a good twenty years since I was here last. Before I continue though, I should like to congratulate and thank the committee for their efforts to make this presentation possible.

219

Receiving the letter has set off two very strong emotions. First there is the sadness of the school closing, although talking to the Headmaster of a Prep. School in Shropshire recently, he was adamant that you need at least 100 boys to make a prep. school pay now, so perhaps it is quite some achievement that Mr. Vezey has been able to continue for so long.

I have no doubt that we all have very happy memories of Beaumont House. I was here in 1946 and after a visit to Kenya, here also 1948-1951. Not only was the scholastic standard high, we were also given a very good grounding in sport and an appreciation of the big world around us. I recall good food with plenty of fresh fruit and vegetables, all this at a time when rationing was still present, including sweets. Then there were the other pursuits. The early morning P.T., the round of golf before Assembly, the Sunday afternoon ramble and evening readings, the mushroom expeditions, the privilege of picking the white cherries and raspberries, and the lovely blue wistaria, which I believe had to be cut down. The enthusiasm of the Rugby Internationals on the wireless, who needs television? The Sunday lunch ceremony of the Headmaster's two bottles of light ale (Interjection by Mr. Vezey, 'One'), the hand inspection before meals, the Latin Grace, 'Benedictus Benedicat per Iesum Christum, Dominum Nostrum.' Then there were the Sports Days, colourful, festive occasions - I recall Mr. Rawlins cutting the grass for weeks beforehand on the big motor mower - and 'the big plunge'. The winter Saturday evening films, the parade of the 'sick and wounded' doing odd jobs, unfortunately I spent a lot of time in this with knee trouble, but however much I missed the games, I learnt to appreciate other things and for this I am grateful. Then there was the Christmas party and games of 'Beetles' and there was the year when as a new Head Boy I caught Mr. Vezey with a piece of holly; was that ever repeated? Then there was the awe of a junior boy, when the seniors were allowed to stay up to listen to Bruce Woodcock being battered by Joe Baksi: next it was our turn to listen to Jack Gardner being battered by somebody else. I like to think that the seniors would have been allowed to listen to poor old Bodell but perhaps that was not to be. I have no doubt that we all have many other memories, but towering above these was Mr. Vesey. To me, he was Beaumont House: he was also the biggest centre-half I have played against, the biggest scrum I have pushed against, and the biggest pair of hands I have ever seen on a cricket pitch.

Now we haven't come here to be sad: we have come to congratulate Mr. Vezey on a job very well done and to say, 'Thank you'. He set out to help build a boy's character, not to churn numbers through Common Entrance. He gave us happiness and stability, a broad outlook and common sense. He gave us principles and values which he obviously lived and adhered to. He was strict but fair. In modern society aren't these all things to be cherished and grateful for? Schools will come, schools will go, probably comprehensive, small businesses will start, flourish, be taken over and end up as departments of big combines, even the founder's name will disappear, but what Mr. Vezey has given us will last all our lives and well into the lives of our children. Isn't this something to be proud of?

So, in conclusion, I should like to say, on behalf of all of us and of those not present, Congratulations, Sir, thank you very much for what you have given us and may you have many years of happiness and contentment ahead of you to contemplate your many achievements and successes and which quite possibly you didn't have time to enjoy at the time.

                    Thank you!'

Next, David Yiend presented Mr. Vezey with one of the gifts, a magnificent silver salver beautifully engraved with the school badge and an inscription saying that it was 'with sincere thanks from his boys' - words which particularly pleased the recipient, who then made the following speech. At least Mr. Vezey intended using precisely these words but subsequently he realized that, wishing to avoid pauses for thought or frequent checking of notes, he had forgotten a few small items.

"My dear Boys, the younger of you might think it queer that the others much their senior should be included in that form of address, but recently at Oxford the senior member of my College, a sprightly 98, addressed me as 'my young friend' and when you have yourself passed the psalmist's 'three score years and ten' that can be quite soothing. Anyway, when your parents did me the honour of putting you in my care, you became, as I have often said, in some sort 'my boys', and as so many of you have come home to-night, and some from great distances, while others, I am told, have written from all over the world, it would seem that you approved of your parents' decision. So I address you now as 'My dear Boys', 'My very dear Boys'! you have given me to-night a quite impossible task - to say, 'Thank you' for these marvellous gifts, for this wonderful turn-out, and for everything connected with it would have strained the powers of a Churchill. In particular, I must try to express my special thanks to David Yiend, Anthony Abadjian and David Eggleden - the younger 'Egg'. The first two came to see me late last year to ask me to keep free the 27th February. They explained that they had had my Old Boys file smuggled out of the school and back again without my missing it, and showed me a copy of the very kind circular letter of which you all have had a copy. It pleased me particularly that the signatories, average age twenty, had seen fit to praise my discipline. That is something our country needs to-day and whatever our detractors may say, the independent schools will continue to supply leaders and so must set an example, 'Save he serve no man may rule'. Kipling, gentlemen, as you will doubtless recognize and some of you will expect at least one Kipling quotation from me.

Some time later, the three of them came along and said that they had purchased a silver salver and were having it engraved. I told them that they could not have thought of anything which would give me greater pleasure. However, they went on to say that there was a very large sum of money still in hand and that they had had replies from all over the world. I was simply staggered and the results of your amazing kindness and manificence can be seen not only in this magnificent salver but also in this portrait and in the summer-house by the swimming bath, and today I've seen that beautiful vellum scroll bearing your names. Gentlemen, you made me feel then, as you make me feel now extremely proud but at the same time very very humble and I thank you from the bottom of my heart, while knowing full well that I am not worthy of such very wonderful tributes. Should you think the portrait* makes me even too senile. I'll tell you a recent incident. I met the wife of one of you with small son who had just had a birthday and asked what his score was, he told me and added 'I suppose you are about 125.' His mother rebuked him, while I said 'I don't think I should be riding this push bike at that age'. The mother gave me a half glance and said 'I'm not so sure about that'.
* On view Royal Society of Portrait Painters' Exhibition, 26th May.

A BRIEF HISTORY OF HMS CONWAY

1859:   Training Ship established for the training of Merchant Navy and some Royal Navy Cadets, many of whom achieved high rank, and the Admiralty loaned a frigate HMS *Conway*. She was moored on the Mersey, but proved to be too small.

1861:   Replaced by HMS *Winchester*, which was renamed HMS *Conway*.

1876:   Replaced by HMS *Nile*, and renamed HMS *Conway*. HMS *Nile*.
Launched in 1839 as a two deck second rate battleship. She is slightly bigger and faster than the earlier HMS *Victory* now in Portsmouth.
After periods in reserve, in 1859 an engine was added with a propeller that could be raised out of the water, similar to the SS *Great Britain* now in Bristol. She was one of the first Naval ships to be so fitted, and helped to transform future designs.
She saw active service in the Crimean War off Russia, including blockading St Petersberg,
The American Civil War, and was Flagship of different Squadrons.
The ship was moored off Rock Ferry until 1941, when she was moved to Bangor because of some near misses in the blitz. In 1949 she was moved to Plas Newydd where a Shore Base was also established. In April 1953 she was being moved for much needed maintenance, but sadly foundered and became a total loss. The Shore Base school continued until 1974.